92   Balducci, Carolyn
De
          A self-made woman

DATE DUE

FEB. 2 8 1983		
OCT. 3 1 1983		
JUL 2 7 1987		
OCT 3 1969		
JAN. 2 1 1995		
FEB 1 1995		
AC 0 3 7		

A
SELF-MADE
WOMAN

Grazia Deledda at age sixteen

A
SELF-MADE
WOMAN

Biography of Nobel-Prize-Winner

Grazia Deledda

CAROLYN BALDUCCI

Houghton Mifflin Company Boston 1975

Acknowledgments

I would like to indicate, here, the collaboration of my husband, Gioacchino, who contributed to this work immeasurably as translator, researcher, advisor, instigator, and patient friend.

I would also like to thank my friend, the noted Italian scholar, critic, and author, Carmen Scano, whose many letters and private papers have vastly enriched this work. Her revision of her father's *Versi e Prose Giovanili di Grazia Deledda* provided me with a great deal of up-to-date information.

I am deeply grateful to Dr. Nanda Madesani Deledda and to her sister for sharing family memories and photographs with me.

Other individuals who have been of great help are Gonnario Pinna, of Nuoro, who contributed valuable materials, Sergio Costa of Sassari and Antonio De Muro of Cagliari who sent me some significant publications.

I must especially thank Signora Giovanna Piras and her staff at the public library in Nuoro, the Bibliotecca Sebastiano Satta, for providing me with unique and otherwise unavailable materials on Grazia Deledda. I relied on the Hatcher Graduate Library at the University of Michigan, Ann Arbor, for my basic research among their fine collection of books by and about Grazia Deledda.

Houghton Mifflin and my editor, Melanie Kroupa, deserve the most thanks of all. Without their generous support and sense of adventure this book could not have been written.

Library of Congress Cataloging in Publication Data

Balducci, Carolyn
   A self-made woman

   SUMMARY: A biography of a Sardinian woman who deter-
minedly rose above the restrictions of her environment to
win the Nobel Prize for literature in 1926.
   1. Deledda, Grazia, 1871–1936 — Biography — Juvenile
literature. [1. Deledda, Grazia, 1871–1936. 2. Authors,
Italian] I. Title.
PQ4811.E6Z58   853'.9'12 [B] [92]   75-17032
ISBN 0-395-21914-0

To Sirad's Nanna, Nonna, and Aunts

Also by
CAROLYN BALDUCCI

Is There a Life After Graduation, Henry Birnbaum?
Earwax

"We know that any person's life is similar
to a thousand others,
but that by 'accident' it has taken a path
that the thousand others
could not and in fact did not take."

Antonio Gramsci

CHAPTER ONE

One autumn day, when even the Roman sun was too weak to warm the air sufficiently to suit her, the tiny white-haired woman slowly entered the recording studio of the national record library. It was 1934 and all the faces in the room around her in the *Discoteca di Stato* reflected the ambition, the empty vanity of Signor Mussolini's version of progress. Her husband, Palmiro, stood beside her, as he often did when she had to appear in public. She glanced at him and thought, *My husband is like a boy, still so handsome.* As for herself, she knew that she had never been truly beautiful and that now she must look older than her sixty-three years. To these strange young men in the room she must seem ninety, one hundred. *A national monument is always treated badly,* she thought.

She seemed as frail as an autumn leaf. She was in pain, yet she wore an expression of courage and patience like a mask as she crossed the room, noble as an elfin queen, and sat in a throne-like chair, which was ornately carved and covered with cut velvet. It seemed as much out of place, as medieval, as the woman, for everywhere in the room there were machines and

1

all sorts of wires and reels. How she hated speaking, and today, only because she was a national monument, they wanted her to record her voice. *It is my duty,* she thought, *so be it. Soon it will be over.* Her dark green eyes relentlessly studied the strange mechanical surroundings and the strange mechanical people there.

They brought her a cup of espresso coffee. *Not strong enough,* she complained silently. *Weak coffee and weak people. Sfarzo* (what a farce), *the manufacture of history. What a surreal, bizarre world this is, all an artifice of past and future. Why is there a need to talk when one has written so much?*

It was time. The machine of history hummed. The mechanical things were moving and the mechanical people were ready with their buttons and microphones. She began, "In Rome, after the turbulence of my youth I built my house where I live tranquilly with my companion of life, to listen to the ardent voices of my young sons. I have had all the things which a woman could ask of her destiny. But grand, above each blessing: faith in life and in God."

That was all she had to say. Palmiro assisted her from her chair and they said their good-byes. When they had gone, the technicians put away their equipment and muttered about how little time she had taken. They began to dispute how best to spend the rest of the day. "La Deledda" had proved a disappointment. Of course it was not every day that one met a Nobel Prize winner, but hadn't everyone read everything she had written? One man remarked that she looked the same as in her photographs. Another disagreed, adding that to him she resembled the Kibuki dancers he had once seen at the Teatro Adriano. Then their discussion turned to Pirandello's latest

2

play and continued their conversation as they left for dinner.

The tiny, sickly grandmother left only a few words inscribed by her voice in the wax disks at that recording studio. At that point she was the author of thirty novels and she would write three more before her death, less than two years from that day. She had also written some two hundred and fifty short stories and articles. Her career had begun in Sardinia, when she was only sixteen years old. Her reputation had been built around her Sardinian themes and her concern with deep, probing moral issues. Yet she was a highly successful popular author.

"When I began to write," she had recollected once before, "was I not using those materials which were at hand? If I continued to use this material for the rest of my life it is because I knew who I was when I grew up, tied as I was to my people: and my soul was linked with theirs, and when I peered in to my characters' souls it was into my own soul that I was looking and all the agonies that I have told on thousands of pages in my novels were my own suffering, my own pain, my own tears shed in my tragic adolescence. This is my secret!"

Grazia Deledda was born on September 27, 1871, just after the first anniversary of Italian unification. Her birthplace was her parents' house in Nuoro in the heart of the island of Sardinia. Nuoro is in a mountainous zone known as Barbagia ("place of the barbarian") where the language spoken was Logudoro, one of a number of dialects found on the island. The town was cut off from the rest of the world, with neither railroad nor telegraph. The principal means of transportation was the horse. There were few services other than the post office. The small school could not accommodate many pupils because there was only a handful of teachers. There were two doctors at most, and a few lawyers. Illumination was by candlelight or oil lamps and there were no sewers or sanitation. Everyone drank well water or water from the streams. There were regular bouts with malaria and other contagious diseases. Ninety-five percent of the population was illiterate, including all of Grazia Deledda's ancestors and even her own mother. In 1871, Nuoro was exactly as Deledda herself was to describe it: "a village of the Bronze Age."

Primitive and forlorn as it was, Nuoro nevertheless was a place in which the romance and drama of earlier periods were perpetuated. The people about whom Grazia spent her life writing still seemed to have traces in their blood of ancestors who had arrived at the island of Sardinia during the Bronze Age. As a child, Grazia heard about the *nuraghe* and the bronze sculptures shepherds had found; everyone told her that these conical stone structures were evil places where wicked spirits lived. The mystery of these structures permeated life in Barbagia, where superstitions were taken seriously.

The builders of the Nuraghic culture were nearly exterminated by the Romans, who executed eight thousand of them and deported thousands more as slaves. The Romans then used Sardinia as a penal colony where they put their strongest captives to work at the mines. Since Barbagia was the zone the Romans had the most trouble subjugating, it was the place to which many tribes fled. These early tribes consisted mainly of hunters, not farmers or fishermen, and their descendants were also fine hunters, soldiers, and horsemen.

With the decline of the Roman Empire, Sardinia fell into the hands of the Vandals and then the Goths, who exploited the island's central location in the Mediterranean for their attacks on the coasts of North Africa, Italy, southern France,

4

and Spain. In time the Aragonese of Spain gained control of the island, but after a long rule they exchanged it for the Savoyard prince's Sicily. After a period of voluntary exile in Cagliari to escape a *coup d'état*, the ruling Savoy adopted the name "King of Sardinia" and as such provided the political and economic leadership between 1810 and 1870 that rid Italy of foreign control and united it under his crown. Despite their official title, however, the Savoys proved to be indifferent to the problems of their Sardinian subjects. The people anticipated this in a popular song:

> *"For us it is no better*
> *Not important who rules*
> *Whether it be Philip the Fifth*
> *Or the Emperor Charles."*

Fifty years before Grazia Deledda was born, and before the unification of Italy had been accomplished, the Savoy government legislated radical land reforms, designed to take vast tracts of land away from the nobility and the Church, and to create a land-owning middle class. This Act of Closure of 1820, patterned after similar laws in England, failed to make allowances for the remote rural areas, especially Sardinia, where the tax-free, deedless, barter economy — not much better than serfdom — was still in existence. Even England had suffered when its peasants poured into the cities, causing food prices to rise and factory wages to sink. Nowhere in the Kingdom of Sardinia were there signs of an Industrial Revolution like England's, nor did anyone outside of England know the secret of British industrial expansion: the conversion of coal into energy. Charcoal was used as a substitute. When

European timber had been depleted the forests of Sardinia — even in the remote central highlands — were stripped to provide the rest of the kingdom, and other European nations as well, with railroad ties, factory beams, industrial fuel, and ashes for filtration. In short, a major natural resource was taken away from Sardinia and the entire ecology collapsed. Cultivation of the land would have been the only alternative once the natural habitat of the game on which the people lived had been destroyed, but soil erosion and uneven precipitation resulting from forest depletion prevented successful farming.

Lack of native capital and outside investors made progress in an industrial direction impossible. Even though the island's economy was based on wool exports, not a single wool processing plant existed on Sardinia itself for almost a century. Therefore, British and French textile companies were able to purchase Sardinian wool for their mills at its lowest value and no new jobs were created for Sardinians. The disenfranchised peasants of Sardinia did not have the option of emigration to industrial centers. Taxation was introduced as well as a completely foreign set of laws. Landownership, proprietary laws, and the use of money as a means of exchange were innovations that came too suddenly to the Sardinians. With the climate and soil conditions working against them, few landowners could sell enough goods to pay their annual property assessments, while at the same time, the Savoy government's civil war made taxes steadily rise. Many were able to raise cash by charging a tithe to shepherds for the use of their walled-in pastures, called *tancas*, even when they had been grazed out and the flock had to cross them only to reach green grass. Even so, many landowners could not pay their own workers. It took only sixteen years before open rebellion broke out. Shepherds murdered landowners, burned their homes, and left their livestock dead in the fields.

An army of soldiers was sent to protect the taxpayers. They were garrisoned in the foreboding round prison that overlooked most of Nuoro. Many men were arrested and put into jail for trivial things, but the crime rate continued to go up. Many became outlaws and hid out in the wilderness, for the foreign *carabinieri* could never pursue them over the treacherous terrain. Other young men were drafted or enlisted in the army, where they fought bravely for a government that did nothing to help their people. The poverty and primitive conditions of the majority of people increased since the time of the "land reform" and by the time Grazia Deledda was sixteen she had heard enough bitter stories of suffering, poverty, and misfortune to begin a lengthy writing career.

Few people benefitted from the land reform acts as much as both of Grazia Deledda's grandfathers, each of whom had been illiterate peasants. The people of Nuoro thought of Grazia's maternal grandfather as a foreigner, for Andrea Cambosu spoke what seemed to them to be Spanish, though it was merely a coastal Sardinian dialect. Having lost too many kinsmen to the relentless green water in which they fished, Cambosu came to Nuoro with some money and bought a scrap of land. He married Nicolosa Parededdu, a tiny woman of Nuoro, full of "spirit" and as eccentric as he. They were devoted to each other and they dedicated their lives to God and to their children. They had barely enough money to send their sons to school. Eventually one became a municipal secretary in another city and the other, Sebastiano, decided to become a priest. In time only the youngest of their three

7

daughters, Chiscedda (Francesca), remained at home. Periodically, the retired Andrea went to stay in his fields, like a hermit, talking to the birds and wild animals that came to him for food while he cultivated his land. People gossiped about him and his eccentric family. He was, therefore, especially delighted when Giovantonio Deledda sent a delegate to his home to ask for Chiscedda's hand in marriage.

Giovantonio Deledda's father, Santus de Ledda, had been a simple peasant, like Andrea Cambosu. In addition to tending his employer's olive groves, however, he had spent his spare time carving wooden statues of saints. Since he seemed to be carving all the time, people made fun of him and gave him the nickname, "Su Santaiu," the saintmaker. Nevertheless, his little statues were popular items at the fairs and festivals held in Nuoro. Coin by coin, "Su Santaiu" accumulated a bit of money. The birth of his first son, Giovantonio, in 1820, coincided with the news that land was available for those with money, so he counted up his coins and then went to purchase a small olive grove. "Su Santaiu" prospered. He built an olive press and sold his own oil. This brought more income with which he bought a little more land, all of which he managed himself. During the conflicts of 1836, when the other landowners were under attack, he and his family were spared, for they had made no enemies. That year, Giovantonio was sent to a private school in Cagliari where he began his studies in Rhetoric, in which he eventually earned a diploma from the university. Educating two sons, however, was expensive. It was considered a true social advancement to have a priest in the family, so Ignazio, the younger son, was sent to the seminary, even though he lacked a real vocation for the religious life.

8

Despite his lack of a law degree, Giovantonio was as ambitious as his father. He modified the spelling of his name to make it sound more aristocratic. With his diploma he was qualified to act as a notary, and he was also capable of interpreting contracts and deeds, and able to negotiate on behalf of his neighbors. He managed the property inherited at the death of his father, and he earned commissions on the contracts he arranged for those who exported timber, wool, olive oil, wine, and almonds to the mainland. Eventually he acquired more land, expanded the olive press, and built a winery.

Totoni, as he was called, was so honest that everyone trusted him. He helped his uneducated neighbors by patiently interpreting their legal papers and by writing letters for them. He couldn't go out of the house without someone joining him to ask some favor or question. Nuoro had no bank at that time. "The bank," people used to say, "is Ziu Totoni." Others with his educational advantages had left Sardinia forever. Most tried to forget that their own fathers and mothers had been peasants. Not Totoni. He remained with his people and prospered. He was a poet. He loved his dialect and his mountains and his people and he was faithful to them.

At forty, Totoni had accomplished much, but his friends teased him about being a bachelor. Finally, he decided to seek a wife. He had a few young women in mind. He decided to start with the one he knew best, a girl he had known from childhood. According to custom, Totoni himself could not propose to the intended bride, and since his father was dead, he sent his closest friend.

The delegate went to the home of Marianna Solinas. He knocked at the door at a time when her father was certain to be home. "I am the friend of Totoni Deledda. I seek a dove of immaculate whiteness who is hiding, I fancy, in this house."

Marianna's father seemed somewhat offended, for he did not respond with the traditional ceremony. Instead he went to consult with his daughter and then returned to the door. "My daughter regrets that she is not interested in meeting a friend of the saint-maker's son."

Totoni's friend was undaunted, and proceded to the house of a second young woman, whose father also refused Totoni's proposal. Then he went to the house of the third choice, Chiscedda Cambosu, the youngest, the poorest, and the least elegant of the three. "I am the friend of Totoni Deledda," he said when Andrea Cambosu himself came to the door, "and I seek a dove of immaculate whiteness who is hiding, I fancy, in this house."

Cambosu pretended not to understand, but invited the young man to step inside. "There is no dove in this house. Perhaps she has flown to the mountaintop."

"No, no, she is here," the friend insisted.

Cambosu left the room and returned, escorting his son-in-law's mother, an elderly woman who was stone deaf. "Is this the dove you want?"

"No!" laughed the friend.

Cambosu went out again, and returned with his tiny wife, Nicolosa. "Is this the dove you want?"

"No," the friend replied.

Cambosu went out of the room again, and returned, carrying his infant granddaughter in to the room in his arms. "This is the dove you want, then?"

"No!" the friend said, fairly bursting with laughter. "It is Chiscedda I want to see."

"Ah," replied Cambosu, leaving the room.

When he returned Chiscedda was with him.

"Yes!" exclaimed the friend, "That is the white dove I was looking for!"

Chiscedda was beautiful. Her skin was extremely pale and her eyes were a deep brown. From the way she carried herself, one could see that she was strong and healthy. To be sure, there was no way of knowing her character through appearances, and no one guessed that hidden within such a graceful exterior was a melancholic personality. She was barely nineteen, and had already fallen in love with a man her own age. Though he was poor, he was handsome and brave. Her parents did not understand. They did not want for her the struggle, the sorrow of poverty. Andrea respected the Deledda name. Though he knew it would break her heart, while escorting his daughter to meet the delegate, he had told her that she would become Totoni's wife.

After a brief introduction all the women left the room, and the two men sat down to discuss financial matters and to set a date for the exchange of gifts. Cambosu was not a wealthy man and he had no dowry for his daughter. However, at the suggestion of his wife, he offered to give Chiscedda an old house left by her grandparents. Totoni's friend was agreeable. After all, Totoni would never need to worry about money. They decided that the day of betrothal would be in one week. Totoni's friend departed with the good news.

One week later, Totoni's delegate, dressed in his finest clothes, led a group of men, all Totoni's friends and relatives, to the Cambosu house. This group, called the *paralimpos*, bore Totoni's gifts: some jewelry for Chiscedda, some fancy cakes, and, most precious of all, a large cut glass dish that Totoni had ordered from Rome.

Totoni's delegate knocked at the door. No one answered. He knocked again. Still no answer. Finally he knocked with all his strength. A voice from behind the locked door asked, "What do you want?"

With one voice, the *paralimpos* answered, "Honor and virtue!"

Andrea Cambosu opened the door, making ceremonious excuses that he had not heard them the first time they knocked.

The *paralimpos* entered and displayed the presents Totoni had sent. Cambosu and his wife revealed their modest gifts for Totoni. The afternoon concluded with a huge banquet. As custom would have it, neither the prospective bride nor groom attended.

Soon the day of the wedding grew near. Friends assembled to carry the household furnishings to the couple's new home. The procession was led by the prettiest girl in Nuoro, who carried the tall clay jar Chiscedda would use to draw water from the well. The women and children carried pots and utensils, while the men carried the furniture. At the end of the line, a donkey decorated with fringes and brass bells bore the grist mill that Chiscedda would use to grind the grain used in baking bread. The last in line were Totoni and his friends, carrying the mattresses and bedding for the new home.

Totoni carried the largest mattress for the bed he would share with Chiscedda. There was already something sacred about this mattress, for with God's blessing, it would witness all the intimate moments of their marriage, the birth of their children, and their deaths. Still, it had not yet been sanctified and, traditionally, this was the moment for having some fun. When the men reached the door, they blocked Totoni from entering. The husband-to-be, groaning and sweating under the heavy mattress, was obliged to use it as a weapon. The "mattress duel" ended when Totoni was exhausted and buried beneath the stack of bedding. Since everyone had worked up a good thirst, the next part of the ritual was a celebration at which sweet Sardinian wine was heartily consumed.

One week later was the wedding day. The parish priests and Totoni's *paralimpos* sang as they marched to fetch the bride. Chiscedda heard them approaching and fell to her knees at her mother's feet, tearfully imploring the traditional blessing. Nicolosa realized that Chiscedda's tears were genuine and she hoped that God forgave her daughter for her doubts. Placing her hands on her daughter's head, Nicolosa invoked the traditional benediction. The priest arrived and Nicolosa entrusted him with the bride. They all walked back to church in procession: the priest and Chiscedda at the front followed by Nicolosa and Andrea Cambosu, other members of the family and then the *paralimpos*, who were there, traditionally, to protect the bride from kidnapping by a jealous rival. Chiscedda wore her finest dress — a costume made of stiff black wool. The full skirt was covered by an embroidered apron. The vest was scarlet and also embroidered with palm leaves and flowers. Slashes in the sleeves of the vest allowed the white silk sleeves of the underblouse to billow out. Her shoes were made of velvet and they were also embroidered. Her head was covered with a white silk scarf. She was beautiful but her face was so solemn it pained Nicolosa to look at her.

It was apparent Chiscedda was not in love with her bridegroom, though that was understandable, under the circumstances. One hoped with every arranged marriage love would follow esteem and respect, and Chiscedda already admired Totoni. But like every Sardinian girl, she had been brought up with an ideal husband in mind — young, passionate, strong — and Totoni could never, ever match up with that dream. His blue eyes seemed distant and cold, and his hair had already started to fall out. He was a tall, stocky man whose movements were slow and clumsy. And worst of all, he was so well educated and witty that he always made her feel stupid. He promised to teach her to read and write, but she knew it would be impossible. She could barely understand the poems he made up in her honor. He had called her his "vivacious queen" in one poem. She knew she was not a queen but a peasant's daughter and as for the other word, she didn't even know what it meant.

When the wedding feast was finally over — for Totoni was able to provide for a huge party — they went to live at the crude stone cottage that Chiscedda's family had given them at number 68 via Su Gutturu e Furreddu. Inside the house there were but two rooms. One for sleeping and the other for cooking and dining. Between the rooms was a partially enclosed courtyard with a well. Very soon, too soon, a son was born. To help out, a young peasant girl, Nanneddu Conzeddu, was employed as a servant. "Nanna," as she came to be called, was devoted to the young family, and was happy to find employment, for her own family was nearly starving.

Within a few months, however, Nanna's little charge died.

14

Chiscedda suffered. Everyone suffered, for he had been a handsome boy. It was reasoned, of course, that he was too weak to survive and that God had spared him a difficult life. To Chiscedda there was no consolation for this tragedy. The cradle, however, carved out of a treetrunk, was soon to be filled again. The second Deledda son, Santus, was born in 1864. He was the image of Totoni — the same light brown hair, the same blue eyes. Two years later, another boy, Andrea, was born. And two years after that, in 1868, a daughter arrived who was named Vincenza. The little house now seemed far too small for the growing family, especially now that the two boys, aged four and two, were very active. Totoni, therefore, set about finding a new place to live.

CHAPTER
TWO

The house that Totoni bought for his family was still under construction when he found it. It was to be taller than all the other houses in Nuoro, which were usually one- or two-story stuctures. The house was situated on the uppermost slope of the town, straddling the invisible line between the community and the wilderness. It had a stone wall built around the triangular property and there was plenty of room for some barnyard animals and a small vegetable garden. The house was a tall, squared crude tower of a building, three stories above ground and one below. The back of the house faced the Gennargentu Mountains to the west, and from it, as from a true fortress, all the roads leading into Nuoro from the valley could be seen. Only a cherry orchard and an ancient, winding footpath separated the house from the fields tilled by neighboring farmers. Therefore, no one entering or leaving Nuoro could avoid the Deledda doorstep. Totoni was also pleased because much of the property he had been acquiring in the zone could be seen from the windows of the new house: olive groves, a vineyard, several pastures, timberland on the slope of Mt. Orthobene, and an almond grove.

The stone walls of the house were a foot thick and they had been surfaced with stucco. The inside walls were all white-washed and the heavy walnut beams were exposed. The cellar was to be used as a *cantina*, for in the back of the house it was above the sloping ground level and huge wine barrels could be easily rolled inside. There was also room for storing bottles of olive oil, which Totoni hoped to sell to his neighbors. There was also a charcoal pit and other facilities for roasting game. There were pegs on the walls to facilitate the curing of leathers and furs.

Upstairs was the kitchen, the heart of the home. Its large fireplace had a stone compartment for baking bread, and several iron tripods could fit over the logs so that stews and soups could be prepared. There was a separate charcoal brazier for smaller cooking chores. A sink carved out of stone stood against the wall near the kitchen window. Cooking implements would be hung from the dozens of wooden pegs in the wall and a cabinetmaker was busy making a cupboard to hold the pottery dishes and cups and other utensils. Above, a huge wrought-iron oil lamp hung from the thick center beam in the ceiling. The lamp would not only provide illumination but a place to hang drying cheeses and salami.

On the ground floor there were two other rooms. Adjacent to the kitchen was the large dining room with another huge fireplace, and a parlor across the hall. A stairway divided the house and between each floor there was a landing. At the first landing a small door led to a storage room over the kitchen. On the second floor were two large bedrooms, each with fireplaces. Totoni and Chiscedda would take one and leave the others for guests. Sardinian hospitality is a phenomenon of terrain and history. Totoni liked nothing better than new faces and conversation and he was delighted to think how many travelers would knock on his door.

Between the second and the third floors there was another landing where delicate things could be kept out of reach of the children's curious hands. The rooms on the third floor were crudely finished but they were large and they had marvelous views. The sun was setting as Totoni gazed out at the lofty peak of La Marmora in the distance. He thought of his melancholic wife, of his inability to make her fall in love with him. *This house will change everything*, he thought, *and we will be happy at last.*

Gazing at the mountains of his Barbagia, Totoni dreamed of the future, thankful that his two growing sons were healthy and strong and that his daughter Vincenza was as clever and as pretty as could be. Chiscedda had informed him that another child was due. This did not seem to make her as happy as it had before. Perhaps she was growing weary. *Life is not kind to women, even young ones like my wife*, Totoni thought. *But the new house will bring a change in her.* On his way downstairs a workman stopped him to ask about the window he was to make at the top of the stairwell. Totoni asked how long it would take to make the hole and install the glass. The man replied that it would take an extra week. *Too long*, Totoni said shaking his head. He glanced up at the wall and noticed that the man had already penciled in the place for the window. The stairway will be dark, the worker said. *No*, Totoni said, thinking of Chiscedda, *a week is too long.*

It was not that Totoni was unhappy with his wife. It was only that she confused him. He was used to women, or so he thought, having had sisters. But they were all vivacious, talkative, responsive. Chiscedda seldom spoke. She seemed afraid to express her feelings . . . remote, unreachable. In the ten years they had been married, she had never seemed interested in the events of the day. How different she was—even her own brother, Sebastiano, the priest, took more interest in worldly goings-on than she. Totoni was at a loss. He would have given his life to find a way to make her happy, but here was a woman for whom, outside her children and household, happiness did not matter. Every morning she attended Mass and returned home without lingering to chat with her neighbors. She sent the maid out to do the shopping, so she was rarely out of the house. At least he could be certain she was faithful to him. How handsome she looked in her costume, with her head held high and her back straight as a noblewoman's. *Chiscedda is a true woman of Barbagia,* Totoni thought, *with few needs and many resources. With a fine big house to raise the rest of our family, perhaps someday she will love her old husband,* Totoni mused as he walked away.

It was several months later, on a late September day, that Francesco Satta traveled to Nuoro from his home in Olzai, a sunny wine-growing mountain village. The town was within sight of Nuoro, but separated from it by a rock-strewn valley. He rode slowly, absorbing the beauty of the mountains, and the songs of the birds. He was no longer young, for he had a long silver beard that grew in the same pointed contours as the icy peak of Mt. Gonare. In his eyes there was always a spark of mirth, as subtle as the new moon.

Francesco was a childhood friend of Totoni's. His silver beard and his distinctive dappled gray horse made his arrival conspicuous to anyone watching the road from above. Chis-

19

cedda was upstairs giving the still-new house a thorough cleaning, for it would not be long before the arrival of her fourth child. She happened to look out the window and she saw Francesco. She turned to Nanna and exclaimed, "Run, light all the fireplaces!"

When Francesco arrived, Totoni went to greet him. He ordered Taneddu Muscetta, their worker who was Nanna's new husband, to take care of the horse. Totoni embraced his friend and led him into the *cantina* where they opened a bottle of wine. Soon they were laughing as if they were boys again. The meal that Nanna and Chiscedda prepared was magnificent. Afterward, the two men remained at the table with their bottles. First one, then the other would give a toast. They laughed and told stories all night long.

Only when the rooster crowed did it occur to them to put an end to their stories and to go to bed. They passed three nights this way.

Late on the third day of Francesco's visit, Nanna went out to summon Nicolosa, Chiscedda's mother. Nicolosa arrived and silently climbed the stairs to her daughter's room. At 8 in the evening the maid came downstairs to the *cantina* where the two old friends were drinking and talking.

"*Padrone,*" she said, "my mistress sent me to say that she has given birth to a baby girl, now, just a few minutes ago."

"And why didn't you tell me before!" scolded Totoni.

"Because," Nanna replied, "my mistress did not wish to disturb your company."

Totoni rushed upstairs. A baby girl was tucked inside the cradle near the fireplace in the bedroom.

Francesco asked permission to see her himself. Totoni nodded and said, "Here's a good occasion for becoming *compari!"* For to be the godfather of another man's child is the strongest bond of friendship known to a Sardinian and it is a relationship that lasts a lifetime.

"Benissimo!" replied Francesco Satta. "And what shall we name her?"

"We will call her Grazia," Totoni said.

Thus, the guest became a godfather, on the following day at the cathedral. Afterward, there was a celebration at the Deledda home. Francesco stood up, first toasting Chiscedda and the baby, who were both in the upstairs bedroom, asleep, and then his *compare.* "Totoni," Satta began, jovially, "may you have great health and a long life. *Salute!"* After all the glasses had been drained, Totoni filled them up again.

One of the guests asked, "Does she have a good horoscope?"

Francesco replied, "The best — the Almanac predicts that she will be endowed with great intelligence, a strong will, and good luck. And it also says she will become either a great sculptor or a great writer!"

Totoni looked up and said, dryly, "Or even a great sculptor *and* a great writer! *Salute!"*

All the glasses were again drained, and there was so much laughter that Chiscedda awoke momentarily upstairs. "Pity the poor father," someone said, laughing, "if the prediction were ever to come true!"

"A good marriage," said one of Totoni's sisters, raising her glass.

"Salute," was the response from everyone in the room.

It was not long before Totoni and Chiscedda noticed that this baby was, indeed, different. They were surprised at how alert she was. She seemed responsive and curious, looking at everything, every face, every detail. She did not squirm in her

21

swaddling clothes, as Andrea had, and she was patient and quiet, unlike her sister, Vincenza, and she was not plump and docile like Santus. Her voracious curiosity seemed under control, even though her interest in her surroundings seemed to increase as she matured.

Grazia was not the youngest child for very long. Three years later pretty Giovanna was born, and three years after that, came Giuseppina (called Beppa), making Grazia the middle child. Since she was especially serious and obedient, she needed the least supervision. Consequently she also received the least affection, with her parents keeping themselves at a distance like gods. By the time Grazia could walk, both brothers were in school. Enza picked on her out of spite and jealousy. Therefore, she played alone. She amused herself with her dolls and the doll house someone had made for her, with each room painted a different color. She made up little plays for these dolls which, in time, attracted the interest of the younger sisters. Whenever Chiscedda overheard these little dramas, she would worry, for Grazia's childish prattle made far too much sense for such a tiny girl.

For Grazia, the most spectacular drama of all was the birth of babies. She had been old enough at the time Giovanna and Giuseppina were born to wonder about the process, but she sensed that no one was going to tell her anything. When she was nearly eight years old, her last sister, Nicolina, was born. Grazia went out to the street and stood next to the opened courtyard gate, bursting with the news. She wore the stripped costume of Nuoro that was used on weekdays, with its lace-bordered apron and white cotton blouse. Her tiny legs and feet were encased in thick cotton stockings and heavy shoes. She looked up and down the street hoping someone would pass by so that she could announce the new arrival. The silence was long and irritating. She gazed up at the dense blue sky to watch the swallows that soundlessly flew above. The breeze carried the pungent odor of the pastures as well as the ringing of the cathedral bells that tolled the quarter hour, but soon everything was silent again. At last, a window opened up in the house across the street and a dark face, squinting nearsightedly, leaned out over the balcony. It was Giuseppina, niece and housekeeper of the Reverend Maccioni. Everyone called her "Signorina Peppina," with a touch of sarcasm in their voices, for she had left the convent, claiming ill-health, and now she had expectations of a marriage to some prosperous landowner. Even tiny Grazia knew that Peppina would not accept the proposal of the poor young cabinetmaker who loved her and who was trying to court her. She and her sisters and brothers knew all about him because each night he could be heard seranading Peppina from the street in front of their home.

Grazia stretched herself up on tiptoe, gripping the heavy courtyard gate in order to balance herself. Signorina Peppina peered down at her little neighbor, "We have a new baby," Grazia shouted, "A Sebastianino."

The child, however, was not a boy, nor was it to be named Sebastianino ("little Sebastian"), for Grazia, in her enthusiasm for a little brother, had invented him and named him after her favorite uncle, Sebastiano Cambosu, the priest.

The little girl turned and went back through the courtyard into the kitchen. Santus, the studious brother, sat at the table reviewing his lessons while drinking his *caffè e latte*. Grazia could tell by his bland expression that the event of Nicolina's birth did not interest him. *Why?* she asked herself, when she was so thrilled by the dramatic arrival of a tiny baby. *What did it look like? Where did it come from? How did it find us here in Nuoro? Santus might be the best student in school, but surely not even he knew the answers to these questions!*

Nothing seemed to excite Santus, however, except very grown-up games with machines and propulsion devices. He was rather elegant for a fifteen-year-old boy; he was tall and handsome with pensive, gray eyes. While he had no spirit of adventure, and his sense of humor was too subtle for Grazia to decipher, he was something of a visionary, like Grazia herself, but he never seemed concerned with reality. He seemed lost somewhere in a world of thought. Even Totoni had trouble reaching him at times. On the other hand, Santus was easy to get along with. He never became irritated with his brother Andrea, as almost everyone else did. Even Andrea's lazy habits and carelessness did not bother Santus, although the two boys shared a bedroom.

Enza, was also on her way to school. She came into the kitchen for her *caffè e latte* and some bread before departing for the girls' school across town. She was dressed like Grazia, in a long striped skirt, a vest laced tightly at the waist over a full-sleeved white blouse. Her long white silk scarf was wound around her head and fastened coquettishly on the left, to leave her hair half-uncovered. She was very vain about her lovely black hair. Every morning she brushed it thoroughly in front of the mirror, and pulled it back into a single braid that hung halfway down her back and ended in a tiny curl. Enza's eyes were blue and her face, though translucently pale, always had a rosy glow. Though everyone would have loved her simply for her beauty, Enza was a frightening presence in the house, particularly to Grazia whom she picked on incessantly. One

24

moment Enza would be glaring at Grazia, and the next moment, without provocation, she would descend upon Grazia and pummel her with her fists. When she could not torment Grazia physically, she would insult her. When they were alone, Grazia was defenseless. Enza even intimidated Nanna who could neither understand nor control Enza's temper. The most she could do was to separate the two girls, but she was unable to relieve Enza's anger or to analyze her problem.

The last to descend the slate stairway was Andrea, then thirteen, but already very much the Sardinian youth. He scorned his schoolbooks and took part in the petty adventures of a gang of local boys. His parents worried about Andrea's "bad company," for they were not sons of people they knew. In fact they had heard that the boys were the children of reckless and unconcerned men; and two of the boys were said to be related to bandits. The influence of this group could already be seen in Andrea: all he talked about was the adventurous future that would be his. As it was, he already spent most of his time astride his horse. He told Nanna that for breakfast he prefered red, rare meat, and that *caffè e latte* was a "childish" drink, too weak to sustain someone as active as himself. The most extroverted of the children, Andrea was also the most spoiled. He was Nanna's favorite, and while he nibbled some stale bread and cheese, she tried to convince her pet to drink the coffee she had made for him.

"You look like a shepherd," she said, brushing his rough clothes and tousled hair with her rough hand. She put the cup in front of him. "Take this. Take it, lamb. Your teacher will smell that cheese on your breath."

Andrea was quick to react. "And he, who is he? I am a rich sheepowner, but he is a poor scrounger, a lousy drunkard!"

Andrea had learned to scorn those who live on intellectual work as being on a level beneath that of his father's workers. Unlike his older brother, Andrea was already a brutal realist, yet despite his shortcomings, he was a free spirit. Stocky and square like his father, but destined to be shorter than Santus, he dressed himself as shabbily as possible, as if he did not wish to seem better than his friends. His profile was blunt and coarse, while his lips in contrast, were soft and sensuous. His hazel eyes glittered like a falcon's, and, as if he were a bird of prey, he wished always to soar, to be free. At a moment's notice he would leap onto his barebacked colt to ride, like a young centaur, with his companions, and his joyous whoops and hollers were loud enough to drown out even the wildest stallion's neighings.

Despite his behavior Andrea was Grazia's protector. Even though Andrea was as unconcerned as Santus about the birth of the baby, a glance told him that his small sister, sitting quietly on a stool with a cup in her lap, was suffering from a new attack of curiosity. The older children would be going off to school and the two baby sisters were hanging onto their grandmother's skirts, the mother was sleeping with the new little treasure by her side, and Totoni, too, was probably resting somewhere in the house. Andrea sensed how lonely Grazia felt. He smiled at her, and just before leaving, he bent down and, as if conspiring with her to do something wicked, whispered, "Tomorrow I will take you to Mount Orthobene on horseback. But be quiet about it, eh?"

Grazia had already been excited and mystified by the birth of the baby. Now, her eyes grew even wider: tomorrow her brother would put her in front of him on his saddle and ride with her, out into the thick forests of oak and pine.

After Andrea and the others left, Grazia sat alone and bewildered in the kitchen. All at once, Nicolosa, the children's grandmother, entered with tiny Beppa in tow. Their abrupt appearance in the doorway, in the midst of a daydream, gave Grazia a sensation of vertigo filling her like a blood-red flash of light and then vanishing, leaving behind only a residue of cosmic memory as if Grazia had lived another life in a remote historical period.

Nonna Nicolosa, though getting on in years, was as spry and limber as a girl. While watching her wash Beppa's little face and hands, Grazia began to daydream again. *If only Nonna were a fairy, like the one who is supposed to live in the* domus de janas *("giant's tomb") outside Nuoro. If she were a fairy Nonna could make Beppa talk.* For tiny Beppa was tongue-tied. Eventually, a doctor would have to cut a short piece of cartilage in order to free her tongue. Grazia, like all the children, was devoted to her grandmother, though she was no fairy nor could she do magic tricks. She was so tiny that she seemed to the children to be one of them. She knew all their secrets and answered all their questions. Nicolosa lived in her own house, only a short walk away. She had spent the previous night by Chiscedda's side to assist the midwife. Everything had gone smoothly, and so Nicolosa, who seemed to have the resilience of a steel sword, began the supervision of the midday meal.

Nonna Nicolosa sipped her coffee and tended to Beppa's breakfast. She herself felt no need for sleep. Totoni, however, had been awake all night reading and pacing silently in the guest room. He had fallen asleep on an old sofa in the early dawn after the birth of his last child. Nonna Nicolosa washed Beppa's face again, and then told Nanna to go out to buy a few things. The larder was filled with food and bread was baked daily at home, but Chiscedda needed a strong, nourishing soup, and meat for the broth was necessary. The little girls loved to tag along after Nanna when she went to the market to shop, but today Grazia burned with curiosity about the new baby. Besides, she knew that with the commotion in the house there were one or two things she would be able to explore. When Nonna Nicolosa went to the garden to draw water from the well, Grazia sneaked out of the kitchen and went silently upstairs.

At the landing between the first and the second floors was the door to the larder. Someone had left it unlocked and Grazia crept inside. It was a treasure trove. Subdued light filtered in through the lattice-covered window that overlooked the courtyard. Gradually her eyes adjusted to the dim light and she could see sacks of wheat, barley, almonds, and potatoes stacked in the corner. On a long table were crocks of lard and the rounded forms of cured hams, called *prosciutto*. Asphodel baskets held dried beans, lentils, and chick peas, and clay jars contained bacon drippings, preserved fruit and sun-dried tomatos. What caught Grazia's eye were the grapes and wrinkled pears that hung in clusters from the thick wooden ceiling beams. She searched and found the forked rod used to retrieve the would-be raisins. Like an acolyte lighting candles on an altar, little Grazia stretched up until the stick touched the grapes and she pried them from their hook. Midway, a bee flew by, and startled her. The grapes fell from the tip of the stick, breaking apart and scattering across the floor like the pearls of a broken necklace. At first she was terrified, but then she relaxed, secure that her mother was too tired to notice. With her characteristic patience and determination, Grazia picked up each grape, one by one, and all the stems as well, and placed them inside her apron. Then she put the forked stick back in its exact place by the door. Having eliminated all the clues, she knew that she would have made an excellent cattle or sheep rustler or even a bandit, like the ones the servants talked about who erased their footprints so that no one could ever track them down.

To Grazia and her brothers and sisters, bandit stories were marvelous. They took the place of the Odyssey or the legends of King Arthur and his Knights of the Round Table. In Barbagia the local Robin Hoods seemed so dashing that all the girls, especially Grazia and her sisters, were ready to fight alongside them, for even the littlest ones had acquired Amazonian instincts.

Grazia tiptoed out of the storeroom and bumped into her father on his way upstairs. Knowing his gentleness, Grazia knew he would not get angry, even if he could see what she was hiding in her apron. He paused to eavesdrop outside the chamber where his wife and new daughter lay. He turned to Grazia, her big dark eyes shining with trust and curiosity, and he signaled her to come upstairs. Had he guessed her secret desire? She followed him and stood on the second step, only slightly nervous. Totoni towered over her, nearly a giant. When he turned toward her, his blue eyes seemed to reflect the sky. He winked at Grazia, his favorite child. Then, a whimper came from the next room. Suddenly the color of his eyes turned from blue to gray. He gestured for Grazia to follow and he opened the bedroom door.

Grazia's small heart beat wildly, astonished at her father's ability to guess what she wanted. She followed him into the bedroom. Everything seemed familiar: the large bed, the

lavishly embroidered bedspread called the *inghirialettu*, said
to bring fertility and pleasure to the marriage bed, the
wardrobe, the bureau, the paintings, the small white fireplace.
Yet, in her mind, everything seemed *altered*, as if the light of
the "miracle" had transformed the everyday objects into
enchanted things, the way water or glass window panes
seemed to reflect a completely different world. The source of
the mystery was, of course, the new baby, who was cradled in
the hollowed-out cradle resting on the stone hearth. She was
nearly hidden by pillows and clean diapers piled high on the
ledge of the hearth. The baby was motionless for she had been
tightly swaddled with her hands underneath, which was then
the custom. A pink lace cap covered her tiny head. Under the
cap was a red swollen face, its mouth already widened to cry.
It reminded Grazia of a rosebud that splits apart in order to
bloom. Grazia had imagined that the new sister would have
pale skin and radiant blond curls like the Christ child in the
painting above her parents' bed. This baby Jesus, held in the
arms of a jovial Saint Joseph, always seemed to turn his big
blue eyes toward Grazia from whichever point in the room she
stood to look at him. The real baby was a terrible disappointment.

Totoni caught Grazia gazing at the picture and assumed that
she had had enough of looking at the baby. He nodded at her
to leave, and she obeyed. After closing the door behind her,
she decided to continue her adventure. She crossed the hall to
inspect the room set aside for guests. Inside there was a round
inlaid table. She ran her finger along the wooden mosaics that
depicted mythological birds. She tried to climb up onto the
soft sofa which still bore the indentation of her father's heavy

form. It was too high, so instead she examined the two smaller stuffed chairs. For her these were the most refined pieces of furniture in the household. Their green upholstery and their carved walnut legs and arms were not the only fascinating things about them, for they had removable seats. Imitating Nanna when she cleaned house, Grazia lifted one seat slowly, observing the thick webbing underneath. It occurred to her that if she ever had anything to hide, this would be the very best spot. Again, Grazia's instinct for hiding things! Perhaps it was not only love of the brave bandits, that put these ideas into her head, but rather something inherited from her prehistoric forebears who once had had to survive in the wilderness and had been forced to conceal their few possessions from marauding enemies.

Grazia let the seat fall back into place and left the room, shutting the door behind her as silently as possible. The staircase itself was an object of fantasy with its twists and turns and the depth of each step. To Grazia it was a steep mountainslope. She knelt by a tiny window in the wall between the flights of stairs and leaned out, dreaming that a cascade of lava rolled down the bluish slate steps. Next, she turned her gaze upward toward the top floor. She noticed, for the first time, the window that had been penciled in. Grazia lost herself in wondering *who* had sketched the opening and *why*. Had the builder drawn it and then forgotten? Or perhaps her father had thought of building another floor above, to make more room for his ever-increasing family, and then changed his mind. Whatever the reason was, Grazia fell into a trance, opening the window with her imagination. A window there would have offered a panorama of sky and mountains. Though in reality it was merely a sketch, dusty and full of spider webs, the horizon that Grazia saw there was wider and more fabulous than any she had ever seen.

No sound came from her parents' bedroom, and she ascended cautiously. On her way upstairs there was another landing in which a shelved niche contained a number of forbidden treasures. The closet was covered by a curtain which Grazia carefully drew back. Some of the things on the top shelf were so high that they were invisible to the tiny child until she stepped back one or two paces. It seemed to her a sort of altar, with its four heavy brass candelabra and, in the center, a crystal vase. Within reach on the lower shelf were coffee cups and teaspoons, seldom used because they were so delicate. The most wonderful object of all was a large cut-glass plate which leaned against the wall. It was the dish that Totoni had given Chiscedda when they were engaged. Since Grazia had never seen it in use, it seemed all the more rare and marvelous. It came to symbolize something to her — like an Egyptian hieroglyph that stood for the sun or the moon, or the Holy Eucharist that the priest elevated during Mass. She stood there for a long time worshipping that untouchable dish, because she recognized it as a symbol of art and beauty.

She let the curtain fall back into place and climbed the stairs once again. At the top there was a small stove with two burners. She imagined that someday, she, like her mother and her aunts, would have to get married and prepare food for herself and her family on these burners. Naturally she pictured herself living in the same house, never dreaming that she would ever want to leave.

The two bedrooms upstairs were the crudest in the house.

The floors were rough planks and the beds were made of iron with straw-stuffed mattresses. A table and some chairs were in each room. In the boys' room, however, there was one great treasure: a shelf full of books. Some were old and some new, some were just for school, and others for pleasure; all had been bought by Santus in the town's only bookstore. Even though it was forbidden to touch anything in this room, slowly, slowly Grazia opened a big book with large stiff pages. She could not read yet, but she liked to look at the pictures. The sheets were blue, and each was marked with yellow points that she already knew well: the constellations.

She closed the book and placed it back where she had found it. She crossed over to the windows. One looked out over the garden and included a view of the neighboring gardens as well, which descended into the invisible valley from which the Gennargentu Mountains rose. Grazia imagined she could see human profiles in the rocks and castle turrets in the peaks of the limestone mountains and their bluish, almost iridescent surface that glowed in the May sun. Beyond them, in the farthest distance were the even higher, bluer, more shimmery and effervescent mountains of legend and dream.

Grazia crossed the room to gaze out the other window which overlooked the street. Though less picturesque, the view was interesting and alive. A narrow sidewalk ran in front of the house. A sewer on the side of the road drained off the torrents of excess rain which fell each spring and fall. The houses along this street were considered more or less "respectable." In fact, most belonged to relatives of her father. At the far end was that of her father's brother, Don Ignazio, the priest who was disliked, for he indulged in snuff-taking, wore a wig, and took advantage of his authority. Next came that of her aunt Paolina, a well-to-do widow with children, shepherds, and property to worry about. Next came the house of her aunt Tonia, also well-off, whose son was studying to become a pharmacist. This boy's father had died, and Aunt Tonia had remarried. However, after one month of marriage, she chased her new husband out of the house. She was a lovely vivacious woman who attracted the best people in Nuoro to her home. They would come to her house to play cards, to chat and to make jokes, even playing practical jokes on one another, and holding masquerade parties. The festivities of Aunt Tonia's household were the delight of the neighborhood. The most impressive house, however, was that of the canon, Giuseppina's uncle, which was right across the street. This house was even more of a fortress than the Deledda home, with a courtyard and two inner gardens, one of which contained a hanging garden, full of pomegranates and roses, with a tall mulberry tree loaded down with its small purple fruit. Behind his house lay the rest of the town. From that high bedroom window, Grazia could clearly see even the humblest dwellings of the poor. The white bell tower of the Church of the Rosary loomed above the low, dark roofs like a lighthouse among the rocks.

Visitors were expected for the baptism of the new baby, and the first to arrive was Chiscedda's brother Don Sebastiano, Grazia's favorite uncle. He was a priest with a true vocation and a pure love of God. Intelligent and cultured, it was his love of literature and Latin that impressed everyone who knew him. Sebastiano had few vices and took genuine delight in all his nieces and nephews, of which little Grazia was his favorite. He sensed great intelligence in her questions. Though only a child, the simplest things provoked her curiosity and though she spoke little she often phrased her questions in a way that only knowledgeable answers would satisfy them.

Thus, when Grazia looked out the window and saw Sebastiano approaching the house, she quickly thrust aside her daydreams, hid her cache of raisins and skipped downstairs in order to be the first to greet him. She took his hand and led him into the dining room to sit while he waited for Totoni to finish his letters. Sebastiano pulled his cassock up so that he could pull his newspaper, *Unità Cattolica*, out of his bulging pantspocket. Nanna brought him a glass of white wine. Sebastiano raised his glass. "*Salute* to the new baby — and to my little Grazia!" he toasted, with a wink.

Silent Beppa ran into the room and without hesitation probed her uncle's mysterious black pockets. As Beppa's tiny hand poked about, the priest smiled, sipping his wine and pretending to read his paper without noticing. Grazia, who also wanted to rummage through her uncle's pockets, decided to put a stop to Beppa's enjoyment and slapped her sister's hand. But Sebastiano laughed. Putting his glass aside, he drew the girls to him. Imprisoning them between his legs, he pulled piles of cookies, dried fruits, and candies from the depths of his magical pockets.

He also drew out a second recent issue of *Unità Cattolica*, the conservative newspaper, that was edged in black to show that it mourned the loss of property the Pope suffered under the new independent government. Just then, Totoni entered, and Sebastiano handed one of the newspapers to him. It was the only newspaper they read, exchanging issues back and forth between themselves and debating the Reverend Margotti's editorials. The current issue centered around Margotti's criticism of a gown worn by a cabinet minister's wife — the gown was said to have cost the equivalent of two years' wages of the average worker. The editorial condemned such extravagance as sinful. Overhearing this line of discussion, Grazia had many questions she yearned to ask, but did not dare.

Pretty Giovanna came into the room with Nonna Nicolosa and so they all went to see Chiscedda and the new baby. Uncle Sebastiano had become accustomed to walking with the three little girls clinging to his cassock, and Totoni teased him by saying that he looked ridiculous, like an old woman.

CHAPTER THREE

Just before Christmas, when Grazia was nine, her godfather, Francesco Satta, arrived at the door of the Deledda home. In his arms he bore a tiny mouflon, graceful and shivering, with large staring eyes, and thick long copper-colored hair. All the children rushed to see him, for it was a wild creature with the habits and agility of a mountain goat. In their excitement they did not notice that Grazia's godfather had not come on his familiar gray-dappled horse and that despite the raw weather he wore neither boots nor his thick *mastrucca*, the black fleece vest that kept out the cold winter blasts of Barbagia's mountains.

The tiny deerlike mouflon's presence infused the house with mountain air and the mysteries of the forest. He was a link with the wilderness that Grazia was still too young to explore. The mouflon, Francesco's Christmas gift to Grazia, was taken outside to the courtyard. The children shut the heavy wooden gates and laughed when he scampered to the top of the wood pile as if he mistook it for a mountain peak.

Inside, Totoni and Chiscedda gave Francesco some warmed wine and biscuits. They told the servants to add more wood to the fire. Francesco had arrived in a condition that would have frozen the heartiest young shepherd. Before asking him to explain why he had set out coatless and bootless for Nuoro, they wanted to make sure he did not come down with a fever. After one or two glasses of wine Francesco revived enough to talk about his adventure. By this time, too, Grazia and her sisters and brothers had come inside, invigorated by the icy cold air and thrilled by the little animal. They had found that he was afraid of everything, even rabbits and mice, and that at their slightest movements he bounded across the courtyard to the top of the woodpile as easily as taking a step. Grazia marveled at her godfather's patience and agility in capturing it.

"My visit, *compare* and *comare*, was not made merely for the pleasure of seeing and greeting you, this time," Francesco Satta began, with the entire Deledda family assembled before him. The children remained still and attentive. "For several days I had been suffering from the torture of a toothache. All the remedies that I tried — herbs, hot water, cold water, prayers, pledges — were all in vain. I suffered so much, that for the first time in my life, I sinned against the wish of the Lord. I wanted to die. Finally, my wife said, 'Go to Nuoro. There must be a dentist there who can treat you.' And, I left.

"Usually I *like* to travel, to see the countryside, to listen to the songs of the birds. This time I saw nothing, felt nothing. Everything was the pain. I rode as if engulfed by a cloud. And then, waiting behind a bend under Mount Gonare, were three brutes, so ugly that they looked like the Judases who murdered Jesus."

At this, Grazia felt her heart jump — bandits! Even Andrea seemed impressed, and he drew his chair closer to Francesco.

Francesco continued. "They said they would kill me if I did not surrender my money and everything I had with me, instantly. They even demanded my horse. 'Take, take all, dear brothers,' I told them, 'and may God help you.' They made me dismount and they stripped me like Christ. All that remained was the mouflon which had leaped from my arms and prudently hidden. They rode off. I was alone and nearly naked, but, that's the way it is, isn't it? The world seemed changed: I saw the meadows covered with the bloom of snow, and I heard the skylark, or so I imagined. It almost seemed as though instead of three bandits, I had met Saint Francis in person. What's more, my toothache vanished! The emotions which I had felt fixed my mouth better than any dentist. Therefore, they are blessed, those three desperados."

With his white beard and his placid face, her godfather himself seemed to Grazia like a Saint Francis. And who but Saint Francis would have been able to coax a baby mouflon out of hiding, not once, but two times, and all for Grazia's sake! What a gift — a miracle, an adventure with bandits, and a little mouflon all for herself! Grazia was filled with joy.

Francesco left Nuoro in order to be back in Olzai in time to celebrate Christmas with his own family. Totoni expressed some concern, for the sky was covered by a thick gray cloud and he was worried that his friend, on a new horse, might experience worse trouble, owing to the impending bad weather, than he had at the hands of the three highwaymen. However the snow did not begin to fall until late at night, which allowed Francesco plenty of time to arrive at home. It was good fortune that he did not delay his departure, for the snowfall turned into a blizzard.

For Grazia, the magic of the Christmas holiday was

everywhere. For weeks there was a festive air in the house. Chiscedda could be heard humming, softly, while she worked in the kitchen preparing the honey cakes and almond biscuits as well as other holiday treats. The countryside was covered with snow, and the panorama of the mountains seemed like a picture cut out of white paper. When the church bells rang, the sound vibrated as if the chimes had been made out of glass. The ice-covered cherry orchard seemed like something out of a fairytale. At night everything was silence. All of Nuoro seemed buried beneath the snow.

The senses were not idle, however, Christmas Eve. The smells of a feast were everywhere: the odors of honey cakes and sweets made with toasted almonds and orange peel baking in the oven, as well as the pungent warm smell of a wild boar roasting over the open fire. For the eye were the brilliant costumes of the women and girls.

The cathedral bells chimed before midnight Mass. Bundled up in furs the family went to church, except for Nanna, who stayed at home patiently turning the skewered meat over the open fire. The family proceeded in a file, with the small children ahead. Neighbors, also on their way to church, joined in the procession.

Little Grazia walked as if in a dream. She did not feel cold; with her fleecy cape wrapped tightly around her shoulders, she was warm and happy as a lamb in the May sun. The white trees near the church seemed to bear almond blossoms. Her hair, electrified by the cold, stood out where it escaped from her scarf, like tufts of grass. She thought of the good things she would eat by the hearth when they returned from Mass. Then the child recalled that Jesus, instead, had been born in a cold stall, with only a few cloths to warm his limbs, and with only his mother's milk to nourish him. How fortunate she was to have been born in such a rich family when other children in Nuoro went to bed hungry.

Inside the cathedral the illusion of springtime continued. The altar overflowed with branches of the arbutus tree, an evergreen with tiny clusters of white and pink berries. This arbutus, or "strawberry tree," also reminded Grazia of early summertime and the adventures she and her sisters and brothers would have, out under the pines of Mount Orthobene gathering the real strawberries, so abundant and so very sweet. The altar was decorated with ropes of myrtle and red berries, and so many candles glowed that the church seemed almost on fire. The long shadows cast by the arbutus branches sent the images of trees all about the church. Grazia imagined herself to be in a forest, and lost herself in her fantasies. Three men dressed as splendid Magi came forward and placed gold, frankincense and myrrh at the altar. The choir sang, and the church seemed illuminated by the Christmas star. Everything was beautiful. Everything was light and joy. After Mass the Three Kings were to distribute money to the poor, and those who felt themselves to be well-off placed coins and gifts of food and clothing at the altar.

"Glory, Glory," sang the priests on the altar.

And the people responded, "Glory to God in the Highest."

"And peace to men of good will," Grazia prayed with her lips and her heart, knowing that the joy which filled her at that moment was the greatest gift that God had given man.

"The Mass is ended, go in peace," the priests chanted. Everyone left, in song and contentment. Grazia's delight only increased when the sting of the night air bit into her cheeks. From the houses she passed came the pungent odor of roasting

41

meat. The wealthy homes smelled of pork, while from the poorer houses came the scent of game — venison, and rabbit. In the doorways of many houses a bottle of wine and a plate of food had been left. Grazia knew that each of these families had suffered a death that year and that they had left these meals for the ghosts of their dead ones. The poor of the town made the most of these provisions, but the superstition persisted because, as everyone knew, the poorer one was, the closer to death one was destined to be.

At home, the meal, the stories, the Christmas carols sung, were all so perfect that the younger children went to bed in a dizzy confusion of reality and fantasy.

Late the next afternoon, Totoni returned from his walk, his black silk scarf wrapped around his neck. "Is everyone in the house?" he asked in a tone of voice that implied something very serious. The little girls followed him from room to room as he shut each door and window. Whispering, they decided he must have seen bandits or a pack of starving wolves.

They were jumping with curiosity. "What happened? What happened?" Even the boys came downstairs to find out what was going on.

"It's just that it has begun to snow and we shall have snow all night and most of the days to come. Look, the sky seems as white and thick as the wing of a dove."

Nonna Nicolosa, who was spending the holidays there, spoke up. "Good," she said, satisfied. "Now you will believe what I have been telling you."

Not long before the little Nonna, who looked like one of her own granddaughters, and who was perhaps even more innocent than they were, told for the thousandth time the story of that year when she was a child — "In the year one thousand," interrupted Andrea the disrespectful skeptic — a blizzard had buried and almost destroyed the countryside.

"Forty days and forty nights the snow fell without an instant's interruption. In the first few days the young men and even the braver women went out of the house on horseback only to find themselves sinking in the snow. Shepherds were blown from the mountainside. Everyone feared that they would be entombed in their homes. It happened so suddenly that it seemed like a whim of God. Those who had sins to confess tried to make their way to the priests to receive absolution. What awful things people suffered — even boys who did not respect their elders, like you, *signorino studente,*" she said, pointing to Andrea, "and everyone feared that we would all starve to death."

"You could have eaten the tender babes as they did in the year one thousand . . ." insisted Andrea.

"Oh, get out of here!" Nonna Nicolosa cried, waving her tiny hand toward the door.

"I feel sorry for you because you are at an ungrateful age!" shouted Totoni, who always found an excuse to forgive his son's jests. "One doesn't joke about these things. See the bloom of snow we have now. Then listen . . . listen . . ." He opened the window a crack. A blast of wind from the valley shook the walls. The little girls ran to their father and clung to him, trying to hide themselves under his cloak. "I forgot one thing," Totoni said, "I have to go out again for a moment."

"I'll go for you, Babbo," Andrea said, eager for adventure.

Chiscedda finally had something to say and she said it firmly, "No, absolutely not. Neither one of you shall leave this house!"

"But I must," Totoni insisted. "I forgot to buy tobacco, and with this snow . . ."

Then Chiscedda's face relaxed and she went over to the cupboard. "I had bought a present for your name day next month, and I was saving it to give you then." She opened the door of the large walnut cabinet and drew out a large pouch of tobacco. And he, in thanking her, said that her gift was better than a sack full of gold.

Dinner was ready and they all sat down to eat. For once the meal was free from squabbles. The children were quiet, intent on listening to the voices of nature howling outside.

"But when there is such a huge wind," Nonna Nicolosa said, as if to reassure the little ones, "the snowfall is not going to be long. That time . . ." And she began again to retell her story. This only made the girls more excited, for snow was something which delighted them. What fascinated them most about their grandmother's story was how people had managed to survive, closed up indoors with so little to eat.

"The worst thing was the scarcity of milk," Nonna said.

Chiscedda told the children not to worry, for she had a large supply of cocoa. This delighted Andrea who detested milk. While the other children did not dare imitate his exuberance, they too, were pleased for they knew that besides the cocoa, somewhere in the house was a reserve of chocolate and in case of extreme necessity, there was even a pot of honey. Chiscedda reminded her family that all the necessities of life were within the house: oil and wine, cheese and farina, salami and potatoes, and other provisions — all stashed in the *cantina* downstairs and in the storeroom above the kitchen. There was abundant charcoal and wood and plenty of oil for the lamps and rows upon rows of candles. "We are rich, you see, and we didn't even know it," she reassured her children.

"And now," Totoni said, rising from the table to take his usual post by the fireplace, "who wants to hear a story about Giuffà?"

The little girls leapt to their feet and jostled for the best place beside him. Just then, the voice of the wind softened, as if it, too, wanted to hear the story. Nonna Nicolosa, alarmed at the sudden silence outside, rushed to the kitchen window. With concern, and even a touch of self-congratulation, she said, "This time, it seems to me that it will be just like the other time."

In the weeks that followed, snow fell in a series of blizzards. Nonna Nicolosa was indeed right. Death and starvation among the poor were commonplace throughout Barbagia. Totoni, knowing the danger to the inhabitants of the more isolated areas, wrote to the mainland for a shipload of grain that his men took to one hamlet that had been completely cut off from the rest of the world by the snow in the valley. Without Totoni's generosity, everyone in the mountain village would have died.

Nuoro was safe. Even the poor knew which larders — such as that of the Deledda home — were full. However, the long snowfall eventually caused the children to be irritable. Their only distraction was the sight of the little mouflon, happy to be again in the climate for which nature had adapted him. Everyone except Santus huddled by the fireplaces downstairs to keep warm. Santus wrapped himself up in thick coverlets and remained in his frozen bedroom reading, content to be free from Andrea's antics.

Somehow the children were not worried about themselves. Their parents avoided discussion of the tragedies that now became commonplace. Chiscedda, no longer able to go out every morning for Mass, had the girls pray, and made Totoni substitute readings from the Bible for the silly tales that the girls loved to hear. One presence reassured the Deledda sisters more than that of anyone else: that of Taneddu Muscetta, Nanna's husband. A crack shot with his rifle, Taneddu was a strong, utterly self-sufficient man. During the summer he supervised Totoni's field hands, but in the present crisis he made himself useful in a hundred ways: he looked after the pigs, the chickens, the horse, and the goat which huddled together under the roof of the open stable in the courtyard beside the house. He even left food for the mouflon, because Grazia seemed so concerned that if the snow drifted high enough the wild little creature would leap over the courtyard wall and flee.

At the height of the blizzard, when everything was covered with snow and not a living creature could be seen, Taneddu left the house with his gun and returned with some game for his wife to use in making soup. Andrea begged to be allowed to go along, but even Taneddu refused to take the boy. The snow was so thick that a shot might go astray. When Taneddu was gone, Andrea sulked in his hard chair neither reading nor partaking in the conversation that went on around him. It was evident that the man Andrea most admired in the household was neither his father nor his older brother, but Taneddu, the illiterate servant. Observing this, Chiscedda tried to tell herself that one day her younger son would change and, like herself, see much to admire and respect in his father. How he yearned for excitement. Even in this, Chiscedda sympathized, for she could still remember her own youthful aspirations for romance and passionate love that her marriage had never satisfied. Furthermore, she had no wish to interfere with Andrea's admiration of Taneddu, for Taneddu was a devout man, with the face of a monk and a good influence. His favorite evening pastime was telling the children stories about the lives of the saints and stories from the Old Testament.

That night, after the evening meal, when the wind shrieked and the snow fell thicker than ever, Chiscedda and the girls sat together by the fireplace in the dining room. Totoni sat at the table reading his newspapers and some agricultural journals. Santus remained studying upstairs. Without a whisper of warning, Enza began to poke and pinch Grazia. Rather than put up with her sister's teasing, the younger girl wisely retreated to the kitchen. There she found Nanna already dozing by the fireplace. Grazia sat down beside Nanna and rested her head on the pillow of her soft lap. Taneddu and Andrea sat in the corner away from the heat, for strong men could show no weakness.

Taneddu glanced in Grazia's direction. He could tell that she yearned for a story. She was so quiet, one hardly knew she was there, but he knew that whenever travelers had gathered by that fire, little Grazia would always steal in unnoticed and hang on each word. Since these people had come from every walk of life and every part of the island, the child's head had become stuffed with tales. Yet, here she was, with her desire for still another story in her eyes.

"Would you like me to tell you the story of Jacob's ladder?" Taneddu began.

"No!" interrupted Andrea.

"Joseph's many-colored coat? . . ."

"No," Andrea repeated. "Tell us about the outlaws."

Grazia's eyes shone even more brightly. With a glance at the doorway, Taneddu decided on a compromise, a fable with religious meaning. "This story," Taneddu began, "is not made up. It is completely true, and it happened when I was a child. In my village winter is longer and more severe than this because we are higher up in the mountains. When snow comes, the shepherds must descend with their flocks to find grazing land along the plateau. The women never leave home. It is so still and quiet there in the winter that the mouflons come down from the peak in search of food."

"Wolves, too?" asked Andrea.

"No, there are no wolves. We are good people and the wild beasts, too, are good. There is no animal on earth sweeter than the mouflon, which is the most beautiful variety of wild sheep that God created. You know yourself that they are absolutely harmless. Yet hunters go after them. Men come from far away for this sport — as far away as the mainland. To me, a man who would shoot a creature so gentle is more savage than even the wildest boar.

"Once upon a time, one of these good animals was so hungry that he actually came into my village, just up to the last house. He wandered about it all night. Now, in this house lived a girl whose fiancé, a wealthy sheepowner, had left a month before for the southern slope. During his journey, he fell ill with pneumonia and now he was in a town in the valley, recuperating, while his men tended the flock.

"A grave sorrow overtook the girl. She yearned to join her fiancé and to nurse him back to health. Her parents would not allow it, both for the danger involved and a question of propriety. The despondent girl wept continuously, and she could not sleep at night. That is how she heard the light rustling noises the mouflon was making outside the house. At first she was frightened, thinking that bandits were outside. Then it occurred to her that her fiancé might have died and that his ghost may have returned to search for her. She rose and opened the window. The night was cold but serene. No snow was falling, though the snow already on the ground was deep. The moon made the mountain slope glow with silver light. The girl could see the mouflon rummaging here and there in search of food, and she could observe how graceful he was. His copper-colored fur shone from the cold. His big, sweet eyes glowed in the moonlight. She thought, 'Certainly my fiancé's ghost has taken his form and has come to visit me before passing into the next world!'

"She went downstairs and left the door ajar. The beast, however, ran off. Then she put on her cape and slowly approached the low garden wall under the mountain slope. The mouflon would not come to her and she realized that it was not a ghost but a real mouflon. She went back to her house and filled a basket with hay and barley, and put it just outside the door. In a little while she heard the ruminations of the hungry mouflon.

"The following night she did the same thing. A third night she left the door ajar and placed the basket on the threshold. Seated near the fireplace, the girl observed the mouflon as he came forward, darted back, and at last came forward to eat. The fourth night, she put the basket just inside the kitchen next to the wide-open door. The beast gathered up his courage and entered. So, gradually they became such affectionate friends that she almost forgot her suffering. She waited for him as if for a lover. Whenever he was late, she worried

49

about him. She told no one about this for she was afraid someone might harm the little creature.

"The only one she told was her fiancé Alessio when he returned, cured, in the spring. Alessio hid his jealousy. He knew it was silly, but he resented his future wife for dividing up her affections, all of which he felt were promised to him. The mouflon itself stayed up on his mountain peak feeding on the abundant mosses and small ferns that grow there. In the milder weather, hunters came to the mountain, and the girl was happy knowing he was safe.

"The young girl believed she would never see her mouflon again. In the autumn, she and Alessio were married. After only a few months, at the onset of winter, the groom had to depart with his flock, his shepherds, and his dogs. That very night, a bitterly freezing night, the mouflon came back. The girl heard him beating his horns against the door. She went downstairs to open it and her heart pounded as if she were going to a clandestine rendezvous. The story began all over again: the mouflon hung about the kitchen like a dog; he would even approach the fire, and in her soft voice the bride would tell him all about her problems. Now she was happy, for she had a companion. Yet she realized that while the mouflon seemed extraordinary, he was merely a beast who was fond of her. Nevertheless, she loved him. She wanted to keep him for a pet, but she would have felt guilty to make him a prisoner. And so, after each visit, she would open the door so that the mouflon could go back to his slope.

"Now comes the important part. At Christmas, Alessio returned. The young wife was uncertain whether or not she should tell him about her mouflon's reappearance. She decided against it and put the basket of hay and barley outside the door. The following morning she found it untouched: the beast had not come. Nor did he return during those nights when her husband remained. Then an eerie sensation took hold of the young woman. Yes, certainly the mouflon must have been somewhat human: he showed too much intelligence to be a mere beast. On the other hand she was alarmed that he may have been killed. She grew melancholic and Alessio could not help but notice. He did not know whether to laugh or to get angry, for someone had whispered to him that there was a rumor that his bride had been admitting a mysterious man at night, someone who ran in such a way that he could not be recognized.

"Again, the young husband leaves. The small house is once again sad without him. The town is blanketed with snow. The bride stays up late awaiting her friend, but without much hope of seeing him again. However, the mouflon, as if summoned by a supernatural instinct, comes back. Trembling, she welcomes him, feeds him, pets him, feels him quivering and panting, as if she expects to hear him speak. And she realized that this time the beast seems in no hurry to leave. Still, she is tempted to keep him at home: what could be wrong with that? Finally, she decides to open the door and her friend leaves. One minute, and from behind the snow-covered wall comes a rifle shot: the beast falls. In the great silence, a dog could be heard barking and some windows opening. The bride has a presentiment. She waits for everything to be quiet again, and goes out. In the radiance of the snow, she heads toward the wall and finds the mouflon, dead, his big eyes wide open, still shining with pain. She covered him with snow, with her bare hands. She cried all night.

"She mentioned this adventure to no one. When the snow

melted and the mouflon's body was found, people assumed he had died of hunger and exposure. The girl spoke of him no more, not even to her husband upon his return. But an extraordinary thing happened. In September, a baby was born to the young bride. He was beautiful, with the hair the color of copper, and eyes, big and sweet like those of the mouflon. But alas, he was a deaf-mute."

Grazia was enchanted, lost in a vision of Taneddu's village with the houses covered with frost and darkened by time and with mountains glistening with snow and moonlight. The fable had conveyed to her a sensation, beyond words: an impression that was so profound that it was almost physical. Grazia felt herself to be enveloped in a final silence, weighted down by things truly grandiose and terrible. For her the fable was a myth of supernatural justice, an eternal tale of error, punishment, and human suffering. And yet, up until now Grazia had been spared any firsthand knowledge of this human suffering. Her education in life, as well as in other areas, was limited. Her childhood however, ended with that snowfall.

Following the blizzard, the heavens brought rain. The warming air caused the snow-laden highlands to send streams of water through Nuoro. The Deledda house flooded, and plumbers had to be called in to drain the *cantina*. The stone walls of the house were saturated with humidity and the fires which were to dry the air only sent wreaths of black smoke throughout the house. All the girls came down with fevers and lung congestion. In their feverish state they dreamed that the house had turned into a leaking boat that was about to sink. Grazia was only semiconscious during the illness. She experienced the terrible dreams that come with high fevers. At certain moments she could see Chiscedda's pale face as she bent over her bed. But most of the time Grazia was completely disoriented, barely aware that she and her sisters were being kept in beds close to the fireplace in the dining room. She did not know that Giovanna's fever had gone so high that the girl had gone into convulsions. All Grazia could focus on was her mother's pale face when it appeared over her. It seemed to refresh Grazia as though a wet water-lily had been placed against her burning cheeks.

The feast of Saint Anthony, the day devoted to Totoni's patron saint, arrived. In Grazia's delirium she recalled only that on that day big dewdrops seemed to drip from that flower of her mother's face. She could even taste its saltiness: a flavor of the greatest pain that could strike a woman.

Totoni's sister, Aunt Paolina, came by to inquire how the sick children were doing. She forced a cheerful tone when she entered the house. "Today is Saint Anthony's feast day, a holiday for the master of the house. You will be giving a banquet — where is the suckling pig?"

And Chiscedda replied, in a rasping voice, her heart irrevocably torn, "The holiday suckling is upstairs in the girls' room."

And Paolina rushed up the long, increasingly dank stairway to the top floor. On Enza's bed, Giovanna, the most beautiful of the five sisters, lay dead.

CHAPTER
FOUR

G razia Deledda's education, such as it was, consisted of four years at a local school in which she learned to count, to add and substract, to read and write in her dialect, and to read some Italian. This was considered sufficient for girls who were expected to learn household skills from their mothers, who would also teach them songs, cuisine, embroidery, and traditional rituals of life appropriate to Barbagian customs. Women were expected to preserve and perpetuate their traditional way of life, especially important when men seemed to become "corrupted" by education, travel, military service, and even prison. While it may seem unjust, an education in Sardinia was difficult to attain, and even those privileged few who could continue were subject to cruelties and exploitation. There were no laws against child labor at that time, and most Sardinian boys of ten went to work — either as shepherds, field workers, or miners. Those who could afford to go to school were sent to the bigger cities since no small town had a high school. They ate what miserable meals were given them, slept on whatever was available, and often had to suffer both physical abuse and inferior teaching when they went to class. There were scholarships for poor or lower-middle class boys, but living conditions were appalling. Between conditions at home and the deprivations of school, it is therefore understandable that a favored field of study among Sardinian students was the law.

Under these circumstances it was out of the question to send a girl away to school. Anyway, Grazia did not care for school very much. She enjoyed the freedom of being able to walk through Nuoro accompanied only by Enza — who walked ahead of her with her nose in the air. This daily liberty was an adventure of sights, sounds, and smells. For Grazia it was more educational than the things her teacher tried to demonstrate at the blackboard. The route to school went through the most interesting parts of town, past craftsmen's workshops, where carved wooden furniture, heavy wool rugs, or decorative objects were made; past merchants who sold laces, spices, or cloth; past barbers, butchers, and a confectioner. Also on her route was the lovely piazza where the most aristocratic people in Nuoro lived — the lawyers, the judges, the doctors — in houses as large as her own, but with all the evidence of visible elegance: wrought iron balconies and starched lace curtains at the windows. Inside, Grazia sensed, there must be splendors like marble and mirrors, wallpaper and velvet cushions, and possibly even a piano. The piazza itself was the site of the vegetable market and it was the most popular part of the city. Upright rock formations jutted out of the ground. These seemed to have been up-ended by supernatural powers, for to Grazia they resembled pillars of a church or perhaps parts of a giant altar on which some prehistoric sacrifice had been made. Those in the marketplace did not, however, bother with such fantasies, for they used the stones as leaning posts. In summer and fall, peasant women sat on the ground with their asphodel baskets heaped with produce. Not only was this a place to exchange goods, but it was also a source of information and gossip. Occasionally a fishmonger would be there, having made the tedious journey to Nuoro from the coast with his small wagon filled with fish. On the days that fish were available, Totoni himself would come to purchase his favorite fish mullet or a musk melon when in season. He would carry home his purchases wrapped up in his large cotton handkerchief.

A little further on, leading out from a corner of this piazza was an alley which led to Nuoro's main street. At this juncture was a *palazzo* which, in Grazia's eyes, represented all the marvelous royal palaces in the world. It was here that the bishop lived. There were other marvelous sights on the main street itself, such as the café with its tables and glass doors, and mirrors and sofas of which Grazia could only catch a glimpse when someone passed in or out. Outside, men sat under the large umbrellas on the patio near the street. Grazia wondered what they argued so loudly about, and why they chose this spot to read their newspapers when they could have done so at home, and more comfortably. Certainly the coffee that they bought here was not any better than the coffee their wives made at home. But Grazia already knew men had a world reserved for themselves and this café was its chief domain.

Along this same street were shops and haberdasheries, jewelers and a tobacconist. There, too, was Signor Carlino's bookstore. Not only was the owner a distant relative but his shop was the place where books and ink and pen nibs were sold. To Grazia, this was the most magical place in Nuoro, for here one could buy those enchanted implements which could translate spoken words into symbols. And more than words, one could actually preserve one's own *thoughts!* Uncle Sebastiano had already taught Grazia how to make some of these symbols, before she entered school, and so she was put into the second grade right away.

Grazia disliked school but she regarded it as an escape from the monotony of her cloistered life at home, even though the atmosphere of the school was still monastic. She sat by the window and gazed through the iron bars at the green gardens and the olive trees and almond groves that stood out so beautifully against the background of mountain and sky. She listened to the whispers of the trees and sugar canes calling to her from the valley below, and ignored the sharp nasal voice of her teacher. Rather than concentrating on her lessons, she would study the tiny greenish birds which perched on the window sill or the copper-colored clouds of early October gliding across the deep blue sky. Even the loud, almost vulgar voice of the teacher reminded Grazia of the outdoors. Her voice was so harsh that it could have belonged to a herdsman who had to shout to call home his stray sheep. Indeed, the fifteen little girls in the class must have seemed like lambs, for they all yearned to spring from their corral to rush into the meadows in the valley or to climb the poplar trees along the dry riverbed. All the little girls were as wild as Grazia, even though most came from families as well-to-do as her own. Others, like the two girls who shared her school bench, were daughters of shepherds or artisans. The blacksmith — an important member of all agricultural communities — had brought his family to Nuoro from far away. At first they were so poor that they had to live in a cave outside of town, like a tribe of savages. Then little by little the blacksmith accumulated some savings and purchased a lovely home and a workshop. This was a common story in Nuoro, where some people were able to elevate themselves from an almost prehistoric way of life to one of relative comfort.

Grazia's teacher was Maria Angela Funedda. She was not a native of Nuoro and people called her "the continental one" behind her back. She was an attractive woman with kinky blond hair, but she was strict and impatient and her pupils made her irascible. Grazia's constant daydreaming made her appear dull to Signora Funedda, who preferred the vivacity of Enza and, later, the polite and obedient Nicolina and the chattering but clever Beppa. Grazia's silence and unresponsiveness did not keep her from getting into trouble; for example, the class was assigned to draw a picture of a peasant woman in costume. Instead, Grazia drew a man. If her grades in written work were not so high, Signora Funedda would have had no way of knowing that Grazia had any intelligence at all. In writing and composition, Grazia was always the top student. Eventually, the teacher came to understand and appreciate Grazia's temperament and treated her well; however, Grazia never trusted this woman, "the continental one" with her loud, vulgar voice and her empty eyes.

When the supervisor of the school came to examine the girls' class, Signora Funedda always picked Grazia as the one to be questioned. The supervisor was a large man with a huge head and dark features. He intimidated Grazia so much that for her whole life she never lost her shyness in the presence of people she considered to be superior.

There was little that Grazia had to study that she did not detest: mathematics, geography, history. There were only two exceptions: reading and composition. Soon she became more interested in writing in her notebooks than in playing with her toys. She even neglected her dolls until she realized that she could write stories for them. The blackboard with its white symbols chalked on it by the teacher became as fascinating as a window opening out onto the dark blue of a starry night.

Her first school year seemed a success. Signora Funedda decided to promote Grazia to the next grade without making her take the tests required of the other girls. This distinction made Grazia so proud of herself that she carried the note home to her father, skipping and waving the letter like a triumphant banner. This was too much for Enza who spitefully pinched and shoved her. When she arrived at home, Grazia went straight to her father's office. Totoni had often had to reprimand the other children when they bothered him while he worked, but never Grazia. From the happy glow on her face, Totoni knew that her news was important. He wanted to please her so he put down his pen and read the letter. Grazia was crushed when Totoni's lips tightened into a sarcastic smile. He folded up the sheet of paper and tapped it once with his finger. He saw Grazia's drawn face and embraced her. This seemed to satisfy her, this — and some words of praise. Totoni found it difficult to tell her that her promotion was being used as bribe. When money was needed in Nuoro, only he had enough to help. Signora Funedda had been trying to convince Totoni to give her a loan to pay off some drinking debts incurred by her husband. Totoni had refused because he had to reserve his money for good causes, not to encourage immoral behavior. When Grazia learned the truth, it was her first bittersweet taste of the fruits of human nature, and concluded another lesson in her education.

Grazia finished her school curriculum in three years and was allowed a fourth year to expand her studies. In the last year her teacher gave her compositions to work on and much reading, and Grazia advanced quite far, more or less by herself. When the last year was over, she was happy. Though she had not enjoyed the formality of school and the lessons that she was obliged to learn, Grazia was awarded the first prize, outdoing all the boys that graduated that year. She was given a special diploma and a leatherbound book of Tommaseo's folk ballads. Her special diploma, the *Onore al Merito*, was conferred by the mayor, Signor Pinna, and her teacher, Teresa Manora, on July 15, 1881. That day, Grazia Deledda, not yet ten years old, left school, never to enter a classroom again.

Totoni consulted his brother-in-law Sebastiano about what to do with Grazia. As a priest, Sebastiano was obliged to uphold certain standards for his nieces and nephews. He had always been strict especially with the girls, and it was his order, and not that of the parents, that forbade them from leaving the house alone. It was not that he didn't trust the girls, for he knew them well through the intimacy of the confessional. He reminded them of the scandals, created out of nothing but idle chatter, that had ruined other girls. If none of the sisters went out alone no one could speculate about them. But, like all children, the Deledda girls broke the rules every once in a while. One time, Sebastiano caught Beppa, the most mischievous sister, strolling by herself on via Maggiore. He seized her by her blond braids and scolded her then and there, so that no one would think that his nieces were free to do as they pleased. Beppa's little pranks, Enza's tantrums, Andrea's attitude, and Santus's lack of spirit all distressed Sebastiano. But Grazia concerned him the most.

She was the only one whose "problems" derived from obvious talent, a clever imagination that Sebastiano believed could only have been given her by God. Fearful that she might misuse her "gift," over and over he reminded her, "Remember, Grazia, that you are a woman, and that you are baptized!"

It was obvious that she was gifted, but it was impossible to send a girl that young away to school, even had a convent school somewhere in Sardinia been willing to take her. Sebastiano suggested private lessons and he offered to tutor her in Latin himself. Grazia did her best, and her uncle was an excellent teacher, for Latin was a subject in which he was proficient. However, she detested the discipline of memorization so much that as soon as Sebastiano had left the house, she would find a pebble, and, in exasperation, would scrape a mark with it on the front door.

The literature professor from the boy's school was a boarder in Aunt Paolina's house, next door. He brought a trunk full of books with him when he arrived at Nuoro from the mainland. Totoni decided that the young man had a genuine love of literature and poetry and that he would make an ideal tutor for Grazia. The teacher from the mainland was not so old-fashioned as his colleagues in Nuoro. He was happy to have a bright young girl as a pupil and even more pleased to be able to earn some extra money — for all his salary seemed to go toward books and the sweet wine of Oliena, for which he had a great weakness.

This young man was patient with Grazia as he taught her Italian grammar and composition. He read the great poets with such feeling that Grazia learned to love them. In fact, she was a little shocked to see that the poetry made him weep, for as a typical Sardinian child, she had been trained to be brave and never to cry. Out of pity Grazia made every effort to please her sensitive teacher. One day, after he read over one of her compositions, the young schoolmaster tapped the pages with his scrawny white finger, saying, "This . . . *this* could be published."

Published! Grazia thought, maintaining an exterior coldness, while a muddle of pride, ambition, and dream churned inside. *Published, like the newspaper or books or the fashion magazines from Rome? Published, to speak to everyone at once, to tell how one felt, how one thought, what one liked, disliked, to tell the world all sorts of secrets?* Her teacher had spoken the one word that unlocked Grazia's secret desire.

One night, the debt-ridden schoolmaster vanished from Nuoro, never to return. He owed Aunt Paolina quite a bit of rent, and, in lieu of payment, he left behind his books. These books emigrated, one by one, to Grazia's house, where Grazia inaugurated, all by herself, her own course of study which resulted in a marvelous, wild flourishing of poetry and brief compositions.

Totoni observed Grazia's growth and interest in writing. He took particular interest in her poetry for he himself was a dialectical poet and participated in the extremporaneous competitions that he had loved as a younger man. He was still one of the strongest contenders. Around the time that Grazia was a baby, Totoni had even started his own printing press to publish the dialectical poems that he and his friends had created, but the venture became too costly and he had to stop.

Of all of Totoni's distinguished friends, perhaps none was so esteemed as Giovanni Mario Demartis, the bishop of Nuoro. The bishop was so saintly and wise that Grazia knew she wanted to grow up to be just like him. The elderly bishop sensed that of all the people in his diocese, only Totoni Deledda would make good use of the library he'd collected over almost half a century of religious scholarship. Forbidden by custom to make visits to parishioners' homes, the bishop often met Totoni Deledda on his long walks, and used these casual encounters to probe the sincerity and intelligence of his friend. Without telling him, Bishop Demartis included Totoni Deledda in his will, and when he died, all of his books were given to the Deledda family.

Thus, between the schoolmaster and the bishop, Grazia had a legacy of books from both the secular and the religious worlds. The bishop's library included works on the saints, mysticism, dogma, and philosophy. There were books by the pagan Greek philosophers, as well as Saint Augustine and Saint Thomas. There were Old and New Testaments, prayer books, and breviaries. The schoolteacher's collection contained even better treasures: Dante, Petrarch, Homer, Virgil, modern authors, and translations as well. Poetry, prose, fiction, and essays were all there. Through these books Grazia gave herself a diversified and modern education. Some authors such as Dante, made her yawn, but others fired her imagination and she read and re-read those books she enjoyed. Enza accused her of being lazy and shunning her household duties. Her brothers teased her rather unorthodox observations of the books she read. Andrea admired her spirit, but Santus was irritated by some of the things she said and decided to pay no more attention to the silly notions of a mere girl. Chiscedda was irritated, not only because Grazia preferred reading to learning the traditional skills necessary to a wife and mother, but also because she was influencing her two younger sisters to take these silly poems and romances seriously. She often came upon the three: Grazia reading aloud from a book and the other two girls embroidering, stopping every so often to comment to each other about the story. Books were something Chiscedda would never understand, though she had to admit that even she could get interested in some of the stories that Grazia read aloud. *What would become of Grazia,* she worried, *what did the future have in store for one like her? Sorrows and disappointments, children that died young, a husband that she did not love? These books will raise Grazia's expectations of life to a level that no earthly happiness could satisfy. And then?*

Grazia seemed to be reading all the time. Her family picked on her, saying, "You will never grow up and you will never be good for anything because you read too much!" Only Totoni defended her, and that was enough for Grazia. When she was about twelve or thirteen, she began to write, secretly but in earnest.

It was about this time that another lesson in Grazia's education took place. One of her friends decided to share with Grazia her knowledge of the biological "facts of life." She was the daughter of a gunsmith whose family were the most worldly people young Grazia had ever met, because they had lived so many places — Italy, France, and South America. Grazia's friend told her how man and woman become one human being in the act of love. Though Grazia had observed the same phenomenon among animals, these observations were never associated in her mind with human relationships or human births. Grazia had been searching for an explanation of this process ever since Nicolina's birth. Her friend's revelations proved that she had known the truth all along. Her own sexual instincts were still dormant, as if enclosed in a bud

64

which the chaste, almost puritanical example of her parents was not inclined to make bloom. Suddenly, everything appeared different. While her companion whispered more of her amazing secrets, Grazia became so involved with the new revelation that she withdrew entirely into herself. Somehow she could distinguish each of the scents emitted by the diverse flowers in the small garden where the girls were sitting. The strongest odors were those of the lilies and roses which she could smell even though they were at a distance. Grazia closed her eyes as she bent over to savor the perfume of the nearest flower. Like a flash something rose out of her unconscious, from the part of the mind that does not reason, does not "learn," but holds intuition, emotion, dream. It was a repetition of that earlier phenomenon of which she had understood so little. It would have been simpler to interpret a dream; again she was certain that this "flash" was the emergence of the fragmentary memory of a prior life. If reincarnation were possible, she reasoned, then she no longer had to wait to become a writer. Now she was free, knowing she had access to every experience and truth of a distant lifetime.

CHAPTER
FIVE

"Why do you ask this, dear son?
Have I not given you life and existence?
Have I not created you innocent as a lily?"

This was Totoni Deledda's own poem, his favorite, one he repeated to his children over and over. It was more often than not directed at Andrea, increasingly rebellious and defiant. Andrea seemed to be waging his own private battle against society. In his final year of the *liceo* at Nuoro, he exhibited an insubordinate attitude toward his teachers. There were other complaints, but none were brought directly to Totoni. The family enterprises were not doing as well as they had been, and Totoni spent much of his time correcting errors and supervising his workers. He began to be irritated when Andrea's attitude was blatantly sarcastic and insolent. The boy got around his mother by being charming or simply by ignoring her. Chiscedda was not fooled but she assumed that he would mature. Neither parent had the time or the resources to straighten him out. At sixteen, Andrea's personality was already formed, twisted like the limb of a tree when it has to push its way through the crevice of a rock. Yet Andrea's heart was in the right place, for he was kind to his sisters and to anyone else in need of help. While he sympathized with the underdog, he defied those in authority: teachers, police, priests, and parents. Too late, Totoni realized that Andrea's attitude resulted from bad company, and when he ordered his son to stop seeing his friends, Andrea spent even more time with them. They were all young men whose prospects in life were limited. None were as intelligent or wealthy as Andrea, yet their style of life appealed to him. They were known as troublemakers. Broken windows, practical jokes, rudeness, seemed all these boys were good for. At night, they would get drunk, ride their horses through town and disturb the peace with their drunken songs. Soon people were talking about how the group squandered money on wine and prostitutes. When this gossip reached Totoni he was upset. However, he hoped that this behavior would pass, since it seemed so entangled with Andrea's need to prove his manhood.

Finally patience and understanding gave way. *Truth, truth!* Totoni demanded, when he discovered his desk drawer unlocked and money missing. He called Andrea into his office and began to question him. Andrea was arrogant, denying that he knew anything. Totoni now realized that he had allowed his son too much freedom and that despite Andrea's natural goodness and generosity, the boy had come to accept the values of his companions. Without immediate discipline nothing would stop Andrea on his path of self-destruction, for which Totoni blamed himself.

He questioned Andrea for hours in his office. The rest of the family was apprehensive, for while they knew Totoni to be a gentle, almost saintly, man, they feared that he would be overcome by a sense of justice which obliged him, as *paterfamilias* to punish aberrant children according to his own judgment, no matter how harsh.

Finally, Totoni seized his son and turned his pockets inside out. Even when some coins and the key to the desk drawer tumbled out onto the floor, Andrea kept on lying. Angered by the sight of the key and the boy's continued defiance, Totoni took Andrea by the arm and propelled him into the kitchen. Totoni found a rope, made a noose, and threw it over the cross beam above. The rest of the family huddled in shock, by the door. Totoni ordered everyone — even Chiscedda — away and closed the doors and the windows.

His voice was calm. "Look here, Andrea," Totoni said, "I myself shall render justice immediately. If you do not admit your crime, I shall hang you with my own hands!"

At this, Andrea confessed.

The incident was over. It was never spoken of again. Yet, a shadow lingered over the family. Totoni and Andrea were suddenly seen bathed in a light of terror and death. Chiscedda was crushed, knowing that Totoni would have killed her son. *Was it not enough,* she wondered, *that God has taken two of my children?* Grazia herself suffered, seeing the possible violence which lay dormant in even someone as good and patient as her father.

Andrea appeared reformed and he expressed a wish to quit school. Totoni consented, for he had complete confidence in Santus who was already living at a college in Cagliari preparing for the university. Besides, Santus hoped to study medicine and a doctor would not have time to govern the family business. Totoni decided to familiarize Andrea with the operation of the Deledda enterprises. First, Andrea was sent to supervise the charcoal pits on Mount Orthobene. Then he was sent to the continent to become acquainted with his father's business associates in Naples and Livorno. This seemed to distract Andrea from his delinquency, but it did not completely sever his connections with his former companions.

Aspects of Andrea's wildness were visible everywhere. The outlaws of Barbagia were his models. The banditry of the outlying regions became a poetry of social warfare, as if the thieves and murderers who lingered in the rocks by the highways avenged all the injustices inflicted upon the poor workers. During the summer months especially, reminders of the bravery and adventures of the outlaws were ubiquitous. The same night air which bore the scent of the dry decomposition of the harvested fields also carried the *stornelli*, or ballads, of the poor and troubled.

Grazia loved these mournful, almost wailing, folk-songs. And she loved the summer — she loved it more than any other part of the year. It was the season of celebration and harvest, when the orchard bore cherries so red they drooped down from the branches like huge drops of blood, and when artichokes opened their hard violet flowers, and when the hot Sardinian sky was so static and so blue that it seemed to shimmer low over the mountains.

One summer day Grazia sat in the courtyard beside the house. The almonds had been gathered and all the Deledda women, including Nanna and Chiscedda, and a group of peasant women shelled the nuts. Grazia could hear Santus and his best friend, Antonino Pau, in the upstairs bedroom reciting the poetry they studied in school. Their favorites were those fashionable, almost scandalous poems of a writer named Gabriele D'Annunzio. Grazia listened for a while, curious about the city Rome, which the poems glorified. It was a poem distant from Grazia, however, as remote as the voices of the young men, while the more colorful and immediate poetry was down in the courtyard in the form of the women's *stornelli.*

These crude songs were full of the passion of profound and ardent love that young Sardinian women were taught to expect. Grazia studied these peasant women intently and etched their features and their dreams in her memory. *Who among these dark young women thought of anything but love?* Grazia wondered. Their complaint, in song, was of "living in the middle of thorns, for having but one lover." This lover was described in dialect, as *a cara bellu ja ses, traitore che a Zudas!* ("beautiful of face, traitor like Judas"). They sang invitations to their lovers to come "suck the blood from their hearts" in such a passionate way that Grazia shared their emotions. She recognized that feeling as something like that which she felt whenever she saw Santus's friend Antonino. He was an elegant young man who dressed and spoke so well that he seemed completely out of place in Nuoro. His face was handsome and refined, and he always wore a hat with a long plume on it and a flowing, dramatic cape. Like Andrea, Antonino seemed to be acting out a sort of fantasy about himself. Fascinated, Grazia suspected she might be in love with him.

At the end of the day, the women would go home. Nanna, the girls, and Chiscedda put the shelled almonds into clean sacks. Then they sat in the courtyard under the stars. They were joined by Juannicu, a handsome young fieldworker who had come to the courtyard at midday to get away from the sun. Juannicu, who suffered from the recurrent fevers of malaria, had found himself unable to work so he had slept in the shade of the house, in a corner. Grazia could not help noticing how handsome he was, with large dark eyes, thick black hair and a dazzling smile.

Like his employer's son, Juannicu was a great admirer of the local bandit-heros. His mind always ran to adventure and he followed the brigands' exploits as if they were crusaders. Petty feuds, questions of honor and revenge frequently resulted in the episodes which drained the blood of Nuoro and the entire region. Juannicu romanticized these tales and let himself be carried away as if under a witch's spell. He raved about the bandits' freedom and praised their rebellion against the laws of society, *foreign* laws, he emphasized. "Today, only a bandit can prove his courage, his ability, his strength, his contempt for danger and death. These are the qualities of Men!" he declared, for within every man like Juannicu, poor and unable to free himself from the necessity to work with his hands, unable to create a better life, there lurked the anarchist eager to destroy the good of his fellow man in the vain hope that he could create power for himself.

Juannicu's heros were two young brothers who headed a gang of thoroughly armed men. Either out of friendship or fear, a large network of supporters protected them from the police. This gang used barbaric and merciless methods in an attempt to gain control of the district surrounding Nuoro. Their two leaders were brothers who hated society because they had been convicted for a crime of which they were innocent. When the brothers escaped from prison they hid among the crevices and the thick forests of the mountain.

71

Their own experience did not teach them to respect the rights of others. In fact, in a short time they extorted a fortune in stolen land, houses, cattle, servants, and shepherds.

One morning, a girl knocked at the front door of the Deledda home. She asked to speak with Signor Antonio and she was admitted into his office. Totoni asked what she wanted. Her skin was pale, her features delicate, her eyes framed by thick lashes. Dressed in the rich costume of her town, she was remarkably handsome. The strength of her character was clear to Totoni as he studied her face.

The gaze of those black eyes was steady and her tone of voice, while shy, was direct. "You own an oak forest on Mount Orthobene that for years you have rented to someone whose pigs feed on the acorns. We would like to lease it next season."

"It is already rented," Totoni replied. "For three years it has been rented exclusively by Elias Porcu."

"Elias will give it up gladly if *vossignore* orders him."

"I don't think he will give it up gladly, he absolutely needs it."

"If *vossignore* orders him . . ."

Calm and still, with his white fist upon the table, Totoni replied, "I have never forced anyone to do anything that was unfair!"

"But, it would be fair. You see, my brothers need a pasture of acorns for their pigs and all the others claim that they have already rented theirs out, while this is not so."

"I do not know what the other landowners may have said. I do know that my woods are already rented. *Basta!*" he concluded, raising his clenched fist. He placed it back on the table without pounding, however, for he had glimpsed the silvery glint of the sharpened steel of her drawn knife.

"*Vossignore* knows who my brothers are?"

Signor Antonio smiled. "Were they the seven legendary brothers, the bandits who gave their name to the mountains in which they hid, I wouldn't break my promise to Elias Porcu. *E basta!*" he shouted, this time pounding his fist the way he did when he sealed his letters.

The girl took her leave without another word. Totoni said nothing to the family, though everyone had noticed the extraordinary visitor and they were worried.

That evening, late at night, when everyone was in bed except the master of the house, there was a knock at the door. Totoni put aside his favorite newspaper, *Unità Cattolica*, and went to open the door. He did not delude himself about the nature of the visit. When the door was opened it was difficult to see the person standing outside. The street was completely dark, but the glow of the oil lamps in the foyer was enough to reveal the silhouette of a gigantic figure dressed in a rough black hunter's costume with full yellow trousers and soft boots which made no sound as he entered the house. Despite his size his step was light, as if he had spent his life hunting wild beasts.

I am lost, thought Totoni, *tonight this one strangles me.* He lead his visitor into his office. The giant's voice was low and quiet. He spoke slowly and prudently. Totoni felt somewhat calmer. Again, the subject was the rental of the acorn forest. The man called himself a "friend" of the bandits, saying the young men were persecuted and in need of help. The giant handed Totoni a heavy pouch. "Here is the money," he said,

73

"Two, three hundred *scudi*. Take whatever you want, Signor Antonio."

Totoni grabbed the man's hand and did not let it go. His bright blue eyes tried to penetrate those dark ones, like a confident child who is determined to find a path within a thorny forest. "My friend," he said calmly, "you know that this is impossible."

Totoni's touch, his expression, above all the word *friend* spoken in such a way and at such a moment, performed a true miracle. He put the money back into his pocket, but kept trying to convince Totoni to help the bandits.

"The only help I can offer is to advise them to turn themselves over to the authorities."

The giant sneered. For an instant his face resembled that of the devil. To surrender to the authorities, to go to jail, were utterly impossible according to their wild code.

Totoni continued, "We shall see each other, one day, and then you will see that I was right. Those two are like two small stones which drop down from a mountain peak. As they descend they knock over others and their fall turns into an avalanche in which all ends up in the abyss. Send them to me. I will convince them to change their ways. I shall speak to the wretched boys as if I were their father."

Remorse filled Totoni's heart as he spoke those words, as if his own sons' futures were somehow known to him. The man of the mountain, thinking the young bandits might be better at persuading Signor Deledda than he, accepted the glass of wine that Totoni offered, drank it, and after promising to come back, departed silently. He did return, as a matter of fact, but as to meeting with the bandits, nothing could be arranged. The young men were suspicious, and laughed at Totoni's romantic sermon. Yet, Totoni's prophecy came true. From crime to crime the brothers and their gang fell headlong into an abyss. They were caught by the *carabinieri* and among the dupes caught along with them, to the extreme sorrow of the Deledda family, was their imaginative worker, Juannicu, who had recently joined the gang and who had not even committed the slightest misdemeanor. As if in exchange, the man of the mountain often came to see Totoni, and, in time, became his swineherd. For many years he was one of the most faithful and affectionate of the Deledda employees. He confessed that on that first night, he had come with the intention of killing Totoni had his demands not been met but that Totoni's goodness, which radiated to all he encountered, had averted the tragedy.

Innate goodness, however, could not avert the other tragedies that were to befall the Deledda family. Prayers and sacrifice did not seem to work, either, despite what the priests said, for destiny — a mystical force in the realm of Sardinian beliefs — could reverse itself as swiftly and as arbitrarily as the forces of nature.

One of the best sources of income in Nuoro was the exportation of timber from Mt. Orthobene. To the people of Nuoro however, this timber seemed sacred, as if some primordial covenant protected them. They resented it when lumberjacks from the mainland were employed by Totoni Deledda to cut down the centuries-old trees. These mainlanders were strapping, fair-headed Alpine men whose manners appeared crude and arrogant to the modest Nuorese. When they were dressed for work in their rough clothing with axes and saws hanging from their sides, like mallets and battle-axes, the fair-haired men reminded the townspeople of the ancient Vandals and Goths who had also defiled and plundered Sardinian soil. In the stillness of the early morning hours, the valley echo carried the sound of the axe blows as far away as Nuoro.

Totoni put Andrea in charge of these crews. He was also to supervise the charcoal pits and the shipment of ashes to the docks in Orsei. A bottling company on the mainland needed the ashes for use in filtration of their product. The ashes were sent by wagonloads to the port where they were to be loaded from the pier onto a cargo ship. The men unloaded the shipment at dockside, not knowing that a fierce squall had driven the barge back to the mainland. When the storm hit the coast, the entire mountain of ashes melted and washed into the sea. The loss, in terms of cut-down trees and money, was a disaster. Moreover, Andrea knew he had failed his father once again.

Work continued in the charcoal pits on Mount Orthobene. The peripheral areas were gradually depleted. No matter how much timber was taken, no one dreamed that any limit should have been set. The ancient trees were so thick and so tall that their trunks resembled massive iron columns with leaves so dense that there was a perennial twilight on the forest floor. One morning Grazia woke up to the smell of smoke. She rushed to her window. The entire horizon was gray, covered by an enormous black mist. Downstairs Grazia could hear Andrea shouting to Taneddu and in a moment she heard galloping hoofbeats strike the cobblestone pavement. Smoke hid the sun and made it look like a blood-splattered disk. Grazia was certain it would never reappear clean and golden, but would always retain the smudge of the forest fire that raged on Mount Orthobene. The earth, instead, seemed aglow, like a single ember, as if the sun had touched it. Ashes and cinders floated everywhere. The trees shriveled and twisted as they burned. Shrubs and bushes seemed covered with blood. Silhouettes of men who had already reached the fire were red and black, like frenzied dancing, ghosts.

Others in Nuoro awoke and Grazia could hear screams of terror, *"Fire! Fire!"* Everyone rushed on foot. Without wasting a second in talking or asking questions, the men began to put out the fire. Everyone worked, but the blaze lasted all night and a good part of the next day. Many peasants and mountaineers came from all corners of the outlying region, for the blaze could be seen for miles. Some bandits risked capture by coming to help. The men circumscribed the fire, cutting down trees and laying them together like a wall which they covered with mosses and wet earth. The scene was macabre and grandiose, with the red-headed lumberjacks and the black-bearded shepherds working together next to the fantastic blaze.

At dawn the wind died down and the flames subsided. Smoke and cinders continued to rise in a giant cloud which only slowly dispersed over the next few days. In the afternoon, as the fire was dying down, the charcoal exporter arrived. This man, a "speculator," was nasty and greedy. He inaugurated a type of inquisition where he interrogated each of the workers, but nothing came of it. The cause of the blaze was never determined. People said it had been the act of some god, but whether Christian or pagan no one knew. The prehistoric gods of Sardinia had been strong; perhaps they had never abdicated after all. Molk, the patriarchal god, had once demanded human sacrifice of the finest young tribesmen, whose ashes were hidden in tophets. Once again, Molk demanded ashes: ashes from the forest; ashes washed into the sea, blown into the air; ashes that were all that remained of the promise of Sardinian youth.

With all these set-backs, for which Andrea was held responsible, Santus's success at school reassured Totoni and Chiscedda that they had not failed. The absolute trust that they placed in their eldest son, however, was a burden to him. He was such a promising scholar, and his marks were so high, that no one doubted his ability to succeed. Not only did he excel in literature but his scientific interests demonstrated an equal capacity for medicine. As a doctor Santus would earn a considerable amount of money, do a great deal of good, and raise the social status of his family as well. Totoni's heart swelled with pride when he saw his son's grades and he knew that the misfortunes that the family was suffering would be offset by Santus's academic achievements.

When Santus came home during his vacations from the University of Cagliari, he brought books and small gifts for his sisters. He talked about the splendors of the coastal city. Grazia listened attentively, longing to go with him, someday, to see the people and things he described: the opera, the theater, the public buildings, the broad avenues, the shops and cafés. Like his mother, Santus was modest and reserved, yet his presence during the holidays filled the house with activity. Elegantly dressed, Santus was a refined gentleman already, especially in contrast with his brother. Santus's pale luminous eyes displayed the same sensibility and good will of his father. Whenever he had something to say, he spoke well, and his well-conceived observations were enhanced by an extraordinary memory. What the family found most amazing was his dedication to his studies and the seriousness of his comportment. He neither smoked nor drank, and he seemed disinterested in young women. In fact, he spent most of his holiday absorbed in his books.

Santus's presence lent further excitement to the household — at least in Grazia's young heart — because of the frequent visits of his classmate Antonino. Though the flamboyant Antonino was Grazia's first love, he hardly knew she existed. His dandyism made him the subject of a great deal of ridicule from the other young men of Nuoro, especially Andrea's group. Despite the teasing, Antonino continued to wear his straw hat with its long ribbon and veil, and his flowing blue cape. Persisting in his emulation of poet-patriot Gabriele D'Annunzio, Antonino would refer to his hero casually as "Gabriele" as if, that day in May in 1882 when D'Annunzio had passed through Nuoro, he and Antonino had become intimate friends.

Antonino's family background was similar to that of the Deleddas. Like Chiscedda, Antonino's mother and sisters wore the traditional Nuorese costume at all times, though the men in the Pau family wore tailored suits and carried themselves aristocratically. Signor Pau, the tax-collector, was a prominent citizen. Though he had an unpleasant job, his disposition was mild and everyone respected his discretion. He was somewhat familiar with the Italian language, but since even the language of the law courts was the Logudoro dialect spoken in Nuoro this ability was considered a refinement, and a distinct indication of Signor Pau's status as a gentleman. Despite this, the Pau household was somewhat eccentric. The family lived outside the city limits on the old route which passed below the Deledda house. The household consisted of a group of small dwellings clustered together in a compound with other relatives and numerous children sharing the property. While they were all civilized and intelligent, the atmosphere was more tribal than that of the normal family, for most people in Nuoro cherished their privacy and independence. The Pau arrangement however, benefited the children. The boys were all sent to school and encouraged to continue. The cousins resembled one another in their good looks and in their sarcastic tone and in their habit of poking fun at everyone and everything.

Beyond the Pau compound was a beautiful vineyard with a magnificent panorama of the valley and the gentle slope of the mountain. In one corner Antonino had a narrow turret of his own, where he could escape the frenzy of his communal family. Thus, Antonino seemed to divide his time between the Deledda house and his ivory tower where he studied, or at least pretended to study.

Antonino was to Grazia the personification of the perfect man — bourgeois, cultivated, and refined, like certain heroes she encountered in the books and stories she was reading. Her early love for him had gone unnoticed, and whenever he arrived to visit Santus, Grazia would hide, terrified by the thought that he might glance in her direction. However, she was safe: like Santus, Antonino ignored not only Grazia but all the other girls around him, as if they simply did not exist.

The friendship between the extravagant Antonino and the modest Santus was founded on a shared love of poetry as well as on other ingredients of friendship — mutual friends, common goals, experiences together in Cagliari, the routine of university life. Moreover, both were clever and original, though of the two, Santus was the more creative. To amuse themselves, as well as to carry out some scientific experiments, Santus and his friend constructed certain complicated objects. One time they built a gas-filled balloon. It had been subsidized by Chiscedda's pin money which the mother gladly gave her favorite child for he alone had the capacity to amuse her. The balloon was made out of paper-silk, and by means of steam heat, Santus got it to rise out of the courtyard.

It was a pale bubble which reflected some of the bright summer sunlight as the wind bore it up and out over the valley. It astonished the whole family, and all the children ran to the upstairs window to watch the balloon's ascent. Everyone in the family and the neighborhood was delighted. Chiscedda smiled, thinking how amazed her neighbors had been by her son's ingenious invention. A few days later news arrived that the balloon had descended gently, without exploding, and had lodged in a crevice in the mountainside. Some goatherds had seen it hovering, and in the uncanny light of the sunset, they mistook it for something supernatural. As it descended they knelt, terrified, and shouted, "It's the Holy Spirit! It's the Holy Spirit!"

Delighted by this report and encouraged by the technical success of the experiment, Santus attempted a second project. He built a pyrotechnical wheel that was supposed to rise by the same means as the balloon and then to ignite itself with artificial flames, like a roman candle. Some test rockets succeeded. They darted up one August evening and burst open in amazing and wonderful sparks, like incandescent flowers. But on the official day of the launching something went wrong. While Santus attempted to relight it, the wheel suddenly burst into flames. There was a short explosion that knocked Santus to the ground and severely burnt his arm and hand.

Santus screamed in pain. His torment terrified his sisters and parents. Andrea and Antonino and the other young men carried Santus up to his bed. The pain was unbearable but there did not exist, at that time, anything to ease or to sedate the victim. The doctor prescribed a concoction which contained a great quantity of cognac. This was effective in that it enabled Santus to sleep. However, owing to the almost constant pain, Santus found himself drinking more and more, and, in a relatively short time, the gentle and brilliant Santus became addicted to alcohol. His entire personality changed. He became irascible and lazy, neglecting his books and avoiding the other members of the family. He disappeared from the house at odd hours and stayed away for days on end without saying where he had gone. The only person he seemed to like was Antonino. The family was alarmed, but no one at the time understood the nature of alcoholic addiction. Certainly with Santus's past record of dependability and intelligence, no one dreamed that he was susceptible to a vice so destructive and pervasive. Everyone expected that once the burns mended, Santus would straighten himself out. And the prospect of returning to school and his friends was the hoped-for remedy.

Toward the end of September, when the summer holiday was just about over, another young student, one of Andrea's former schoolmates, began to haunt the Deledda house. He was a slender young man, intense, restless, and mistrustful. Though he was extremely proud and ambitious, he was excessively serious. Gionmario Mesina was also from a mixed background like the Deleddas, part peasant, part middle-class. The Mesinas prided themselves on their ancestry which they could trace back for centuries, all of them in Nuoro. Unlike the confused but lively commune that Antonino came from, Gionmario's home, shut inside a courtyard, was as eerie and forbidding as a prison. The family members — even the sister who was one of the most beautiful young women in the town — were so rigidly solemn that no one felt comfortable in their presence. To send Gionmario only as far as the University of Cagliari, the family had to scrimp and sacrifice. As if forced by some obligation to repay his parents, Gionmario pushed himself beyond his limits to gain the highest marks.

Those evenings when Gionmario would drop by, he claimed to be looking for Andrea, even though he knew that his friend habitually went out every night. He then found some excuse to linger with the girls. He entertained them all with the local news and conversation, and enchanted both Grazia and Enza. Enza was then fifteen years old, and already something of a young lady, but she had not outgrown her strange behavior, however. At times she would be withdrawn and silent; at others, her gaiety was caustic and wild. She continued to behave selfishly toward her sisters and occasionally she would be seized with slight epileptic fits.

Both Gionmario and Enza had flawed personalities, and showed signs of mental disturbance. Yet, they were attracted to each other and they fell in love. While Enza was not too young to think about marriage, Gionmario was still in school and several years would have to pass before he would be able to begin a family. Afraid of the natural consequences of long engagements, and hoping for a better match for Enza, Chiscedda forbade Enza to see Gionmario as soon as she detected a growing attachment between the two. However, they found ways of seeing one another in secret.

When Gionmario returned to school he and Enza wrote to each other. Enza's affection seemed to inspire Gionmario and he studied with even greater perseverance. Passing his examinations after only two years of college, he enrolled immediately in the law school of the University of Cagliari. He drove himself to complete his education as quickly as possible in order that he and Enza might be married. However, the pressures of school as well as his awareness of the Deledda family's disapproval undermined his stability. He became tense, morose, bitter. His appearance changed: his eyes became bloodshot and his voice, harsh, like an old man's.

To Grazia it seemed as though everyone she knew was suddenly becoming old. Even Chiscedda, whose figure was still slender and straight, seemed tired and apprehensive, worn out by her anxiety for her elder daughters, and both her sons. Andrea found it difficult to resist the temptations his position and wealth presented him. Santus, who appeared to have recovered, and had returned to school, seemed cracked, permanently damaged like a heavy procelain vase after a slight slip, still able to remain whole, but flawed and useless, nevertheless.

CHAPTER SIX

"D ream, dream, distant castles, along the Bosphorus,"
Grazia wrote in her first poem, written in the blazing
heat of a July afternoon. She was fifteen, dreaming of a
perfect lover, one who would take her to distant places, one
who would drift with her in a bark along the mirrored surface
of the narrow channel which divides Asia from Europe. How
she wanted to travel, like her brothers.

Totoni was growing old and weary, and business matters
taxed his energy. Though Andrea was still half-wild, he
enjoyed traveling and meeting people. When he returned
from Rome or Naples, what stories he told! He described the
stylish ladies he had seen strolling along the boulevards. He
even brought fashion magazines back with him to show his
sisters, for he knew their small pleasures. One of these journals
became the girls' favorite. It was called *Ultima Moda* ("the
latest vogue"), and it incorporated other features besides
clothing: articles on cultural events and books, as well as
excellent fiction and poetry. Enza gazed longingly at the
drawings of wedding gowns, and Beppa and Nicolina complained that no craftsman in Nuoro could ever copy the fine

hats, gloves, and shoes illustrated in the magazines. To Grazia, however, nothing mattered but the stories and poems. They were simple romances, about young women like herself, who searched for love and happiness. There was one thing about the stories that both intrigued and irritated her. All dealt with city women, city lovers, city sounds. In Grazia's mind, Rome became synonymous with literature just as Antonino's presence there at the university had already made it synonymous with love.

Antonino's family was wealthy enough to support him in the capital where he was studying literature. Grazia was not the only one who missed him. Santus, too, suffered from the separation, and lost among less loyal companions, he resumed his drinking. When he wrote home to ask for more money than he needed, Totoni suspected what he was up to. Rather than order him to return to a town where there was almost nothing to do *but* drink and get into trouble, his parents prayed that he would straighten himself out and that by some miracle he would manage to graduate with a medical degree.

Once the worlds of current fashion and light fiction had been introduced into the Deledda household by *Ultima Moda*, the girls became dissatisfied. The magazine lectured on elegance, beauty, manners. There was no practical application for any of this in Nuoro, as even the girls themselves knew. Grazia gazed into her mirror, disappointed to find that she was not the willowy, aristocratic young lady the magazine glorified. She was tiny, with a small bust, a round face, and a blunt nose. On the other hand, she realized that her beautiful wavy black hair, her pale velvety complexion, her soft mouth, and especially her large almond-shaped eyes made her attractive, if not actually beautiful. If anything flawed Grazia's appearance, it was not any physical defect, but rather her imposing, almost frightening glare. Her eyes were large, at times golden, at times greenish, sometimes deep brown depending on the light. Enhancing their disproportionate size were thick eyelashes, and, inside the iris, around the pupil, was a second rim of dark brown pigment, making her eyes seem constantly dilated, like a startled deer or rabbit. This, combined with Grazia's habitual minute examination of every detail around her, led others to suspect that she could strip away every small self-deceit to expose each secret thought and every silent vice.

Grazia despaired of ever being beautiful enough to attract the attention of Antonino during the brief summer weeks when he returned to Nuoro to be with his family. Her thoughts turned to him constantly, yet she did not know how to define her feelings. She wondered if she would ever receive secret love letters like those Gionmario contrived to send Enza by way of his sisters. Even so, Grazia didn't associate Antonino with marriage. Though he was handsome and conceited, Antonino did not come close to her ideal, for Grazia's concept of a "real man" was her irresponsible, prodigal brother Andrea.

While Andrea may have been exasperated by school and by the "bookish" people he mocked, he sympathized with the underdog. He was rather proud of his young sister who talked about books all the time. Her ability in writing had been inherited from her father, and there seemed no harm in her writing for pleasure. She expressed some curiosity about the shepherds and their ballads and folktales, and Andrea invited her to accompany him whenever he rode out to supervise his men. These excursions by horseback delighted Grazia. She pestered him with many amusing questions about this and that, which he, to tell the truth, was flattered to be able to answer. Seated behind Andrea with her arms clasped about him as they galloped, Grazia learned the names of every creature, every plant, every bird, every insect, which inhabited the wild. Andrea knew them all, even the species so rare that mainlanders thought they were mythological.

On one of these excursions, Andrea and Grazia were accompanied by a group of Andrea's friends. They rode out through the valley and to the heights of Mount Badia, where shepherds grazed the Deleddas' flocks. The others dismounted and began preparing for the banquet they would enjoy later in the day. They dug a pit, piled it high with pieces of juniper, mastic, and olive wood, and then fashioned a rotisserie out of sticks. A lamb was butchered, skinned, and skewered, and each of the young men took turns turning the meat over the open fire. The wonderful scent of the burning wood combined with the wilderness and made everything seem extraordinary to Grazia. She wandered away from the clearing, and climbed up to the peak of the mountain. She was so high up that, for the first time in her life, Grazia actually saw the green shores of the Mediterranean. She had always anticipated that the first view of the sea would be exhilarating. Instead, dwarfed by the centuries-old holm-oaks, surrounded by thick bushes of mastic, jay birds, hawks and falcons, thistles and scorched rocks, she felt humble. The graceful undulations of nature, the clear blue of the sky slowly intensified with the slow descent of the afternoon sun as she watched. She was the true daughter of nature, wed to the soil and the air, yet the notions of *Ultima Moda* reached her, even there. She imagined that she was a medieval princess pacing the balustrade of an ancient castle awaiting the first glimpse of her crusader-prince when he returned from the East.

When it was time for the meal, Grazia returned to the group of young men. Everyone else sat on the ground where cheeses, fruit, and scores of wine bottles had been spread out. Andrea made a seat out of his saddle and knapsack for Grazia. He offered her the most succulent parts of the lamb, the heel of the cheese that had been toasted over the fire, and even the tender grapes that he had brought especially for her. The other young men found these gallantries amusing. They had never seen Andrea's gentler side before. They poked each other in the ribs and then in unison, without a smile, they stretched out their own long wooden forks toward Grazia, in mockery of Andrea's gestures. She blushed, humiliated by the rude behavior of her brother's friends, and piqued with Andrea for having exposed her to ridicule. As soon as the attention of the group had been diverted, Grazia leapt from the saddle as if she were dismounting from a galloping stallion. She ran back up to the crest of the mountain, back to the spot from which she could view the sea — green and luminous in the distance — perhaps for the last time. Waving her arms over her head like an eagle about to take flight, barely touching the tips of the ferns, blackthorns, heather, and spike-lavender she raced to the top. Certain that no one but the goats could see her, she stretched her arms upward to the sky and she swore to God, to her heart and to the very goats, that one day, quite soon, she would cross that sea, to live forever on the other shore, dancing arm in arm with her Prince Charming in the enchanted gardens of *Ultima Moda* with her hair free and intertwined with multicolored veils, and that she would become the greatest writer in Italy!

Grazia halted her crazy waltz, stunned by the seriousness of her own vow. She heard a piercing cry and thought that nature itself was expressing its disapproval of her audacity. *The greatest writer in Italy, indeed!* the sky and the earth seemed to whine. The sound came again. It was only Andrea and his friends, signaling her that it was time to leave. The shepherds, too, were calling their sheep and all these noises vibrated and echoed against the rocks. As Grazia gazed eastward, the granite precipices and crevices of the panorama reflected the vibrant hues of the blazing sunset behind her, making the sky seem on fire. The dazed Grazia stood still, like a small goat torn between leaping from rock to rock and thence to freedom, and, domesticated by a lifetime of obedience, feeling equally compelled to return to the flock. Another, sharper, more insistent whistle pierced the air. It was Andrea, summoning her, warning her not to abuse his indulgence. The laughter of his companions bitterly reminded her that her independence would not be tolerated a second time according to the rules of the society in which she was doomed to live. She knew she had to go. Once again, however, she shook her arms out toward the distant sea, seemingly able to brush the waves. She felt like a migratory bird that instinctively knows in which direction lies the warmest, safest habor.

The ride back to Nuoro in the sunset and dusk was filled with thoughts of the future: Rome, fame, the glitter of a cosmopolitan life. When she arrived home, she shut herself in her bedroom and studied the illustrations and stories in the issues of *Ultima Moda*. She studied the pictures of the avenues, the theaters, the historic monuments, the palaces. Rome was her goal, she knew it. More than knowing it in her mind, she seemed to feel it both physically and spiritually. She did not know yet how she would manage to get there. There was no hope, no chance, not even the illusion of a marriage that would have taken her there. Yet she felt that she would one day. It was no mundane ambition, however; Rome did not attract her because of its wealth and splendors. Rather she thought of it as a kind of holy city, for not only was it a Jerusalem of the arts, but it was the home of the Pope. Rome, therefore, was a place where one could be nearer to glory and to God as well.

Grazia put aside her copies of *Ultima Moda* and sat by her window at her small desk. She thought about the stories she had read. Perhaps it was not difficult to write. The events of that day, her feelings about Antonino, his presence in Rome, and her desire to be there with him fused with the pathetic romance of Enza and Gionmario becoming the threads out of which she wove her first story, "Sangue Sardo" ("Sardinian Blood").

The story was about Ela, a girl who loved a young man enamored of Ela's sister Maria. The setting of the story, as it begins, is by the same dark green sea that Grazia longed to cross. The sun sets and a storm approaches, but Ela, hidden by the shadows of the palisade of the shore, is lost in her own diabolical thoughts. She thinks she hears a distant voice calling her. "Only then did the shadow within the crevice move. She started, as if awakened from a deep dream . . . She extended her arms, the small white, tapered hands toward the sky that glistened with blood, toward the sea which reflected the gleam of the sky, and with a sublime, tragic gesture, slowly murmured, 'Before you, Sea, tumultuous like my heart, before you, Sky, cloudy like my life, before you, my homeland's

91

mountains, veiled by fog like my soul, I swear . . .' " and the rest of Ela's words are swallowed up by the waves while the girl herself scrambles up the cliff, disappearing behind fog and the shadows of the great mastic bushes that appeared blackish in the ardent dusk. As the story unfolds, Ela pushes Lorenzo from the top of that cliff in a jealous rage. Grazia ended the story, however, with a twist — instead of being punished, Ela simply disappears — and stated that rumors say she became a nun, others claim she had married.

The story was short and fit easily into an envelope that Grazia took from her father's office when no one was looking. Without really thinking about what she was doing, and without consulting anyone, Grazia mailed the story to *Ultima Moda*. The story was accompanied by a letter expressing her ambitions, her humble background, and her youth. The editors accepted her story and it was published in two parts in the July 1 and the July 8, 1887, issues. When they wrote Grazia, they even invited her to contribute more of her work in the future.

It seemed like a dream. When the story was published and she saw her name in print, her ego underwent a tremendous flowering. She seemed to be having some sort of hallucination. "Grazia Deledda." The story bore her name, printed in black, alive and alarming. *Is it I, this one?* she thought. *No, not me, the little, the secret, the almost mysterious writer: this name is an echo of my mind, which reverberated from an infinite distance, from those mountains, that sea still unknown to me. It is merely an echo of that scream I had released from Mount Badia, that had somehow expanded itself across that immensity.*

However, that first moment of glory was brief. It was not long before other Nuorese who read *Ultima Moda* saw her story. It shocked them. They took the story literally and accused Grazia of having an evil mind. Besides, everyone knew the story of the murdered Lorenzo, for it was a local scandal not long before. Grazia had not even troubled to change the names of her subjects. There were many theories floating about: that there was a mistake, that the name written there was not that of the Grazia Deledda of Nuoro, or that something had become confused and her name appeared in print under someone else's story, or that in fact Grazia had plagiarized the entire thing. People were angry for two reasons: first, the story was violent, and second, Grazia had presumed too much, if indeed she had authored the story as she claimed, for who was she but just a local girl with no diploma to *qualify* her to write. A more subtle violation of the unwritten laws of Barbagia occurred, not so much because a woman was not supposed to write, per se, but because women were not supposed to try anything *new*. The demoralization of the Sardinian people had increased during Grazia's childhood, and as more and more changes were being made in the social fibre, pressure increased on the female half of the population to retain their old ways, for men's sporadic schooling, their frequent brushes with police, their usefulness to the army, and their chronic unemployment threatened to change them into the foreigners they had always detested.

Grazia had unwittingly made herself the scapegoat. Chiscedda was gravely disturbed. Totoni was apprehensive, but supportive. Enza said nothing, suspecting that Grazia had written the story simply out of jealousy or spite. Even Andrea was shaken, for Grazia had not confided in him, nor used a pseudonym. Two of Chiscedda's cousins, spinster aunts to the Deledda children, rushed to the house after they had burnt the "corrupted" magazine that, they declared, offended common people with its display of worldly extravagance and vanity. The aunts heaped the blame on Chiscedda, venomously criticizing her for having raised a vicious, sinful girl, one who, because of her folly, would never marry. They warned of dire consequences unless Grazia were forced to stop. Totoni intervened, defending Grazia and praising the quality of her writing. After some of the furor had died down, Andrea advised his sister to write no more love stories. He argued that with her limited experience, on top of making her appear already corrupted, the story could not possibly be true-to-life.

With the possible exception of Totoni, not a single member of the family wished her to continue to publish. Not only because she was still considered a child, but because it did not look well for a girl from a good family to defy convention. Any contact with the outside world invited criticism from all sides. She could look no one in the face. Besides, without telling anyone, she had already submitted a second story, "Remigia Helder," to *Ultima Moda* and she knew that she would have to face another wave of criticism when the August 19 issue of the magazine reached Nuoro.

Perhaps if someone outside the family — a teacher at the boys' school, or a priest — had defended Grazia's work, the attacks would have been silenced. Worse than the criticism, however, was Grazia's lack of guidance, either from a teacher or from some other local writer. Left to her own devices, she submitted her work for publication too soon, and she was encouraged by the readiness of editors to use her stories. Not long after the publication of her first two tragic romances, *Paradiso dei Bambini* ("children's paradise"), a magazine for younger readers, owned by Perino, the same company that published *Ultima Moda*, serialized Grazia's work, "Sulla montagna" ("On the mountain"), in three parts during October and November. In addition, a longer work was already in progress at *Ultima Moda*, a novel, *Memorie di Fernanda* which appeared in serial form between September and June. One publisher in Milan collected other stories by Grazia, which had first appeared in *Paradiso dei Bambini* and printed them in a volume that came out in 1890, entitled *Nell'azzurro* ("In the blue"). in every instance, her only payment was the satisfaction of seeing her name in print.

What little encouragement Grazia received came mostly from the editors with whom she dealt. Certainly part of her appeal was her youth as well as the novelty of being a native Sardinian writing about her homeland. (As yet few Sardinians had contributed to Italian literature, and the island was the least known, wildest zone of the entire country.) Grazia struggled, not only in facing criticism and gossip, but even in writing clearly. She had to look up many Italian words in the dictionary, for her native language was her Logudoro dialect. Nevertheless, Grazia persisted. Her tenacity, more than anything else, made her a writer. She persisted long enough to master the language, the techniques, and the organization of a true writer. Even so, she had to endure the humiliation of making her mistakes in public.

Gradually Grazia's plots became less flamboyant. As she matured, her focus shortened and simplified. Her stories came closer and closer to home. "Amo" ("I love"), a poem written in 1889, reflects her increasing appreciation of her native natural environment, for:

. . . the sad winter nights
all phantasm, all tempest,
nights of horror, infernal nights
but so beautiful

. . . white summer nights
all mystery, all murmuring
nights of love, of serenade
of azure dream!

full of lovely rhythmic ghosts,
women, fate, horsemen,
brown wilderness, bewitched
black castles.

. . . the strident blast of wind
birds which lightly sing,
. . . the pale color of silver
the sweet song.

. . . stories sorrowfully told
up on the mountains by the lone shepherd
. . . the sweetness of the guitar
nights of love!

. . . the rising sun, blond
behind the profile of the mountain
. . . the silent aura, profound
the countryside.

the night, light, yellow,
its mantle stuffed with stars
when each flower, each butterfly
lets his song fly.

. . . the church, strict and beautiful
full of marble, brown arches
Madonnas with sunbeams and stars
crowned.

. . . tombs in the cemeteries
death, turning in the weighty gloom
lost among the flowers, destined to
think of another world.

. . . stars in the firmament
worlds, mysteries, errant souls
golden stars, the confidants of
mournful lovers.

. . . the secret of the forest
. . . the green open hills
the ivy clinging to the walls
of ancient towers.

. . . the solemn tanned shepherd
whose nocturnal song slowly drifts
from the woods and tells of the hate and love
of the legendary Sards.

. . . my homeland's azure sky
the azure deserted sea,
of silver spume, covered with seaweed
like a veil.

I love the solemn Angelus of night
the ancient peal of holy bells.
which invites the heart to pray
Salve, O Maria!

> *. . . I love my strong, beautiful, unhappy*
> *Sardinian land . . .*
> *But over all, from my heart,*
> *in profound secret*
> *I love thee, O Beloved, with a love immense,*
> *Eternal.*

With Grazia's attention now focused on her natural environment, her new range included stories of the common people, simple folktales, superstitions, traditions. It took her quite some time to reconcile her more sophisticated romantic impulses and the simple stories she heard as part of everyday life. In 1890, under a pseudonym, Ilia di Saint Ismael, she wrote another novel, entitled *Stella d'oriente* ("Eastern Star"), which was serialized in the largest Sardinian daily newspaper, *L'Avvenire di Sardegna.* Since it was not published in book form for another year, Grazia escaped the serious, often harsh criticism of professional reviewers until she was twenty. By then she was a veteran writer who was invited to contribute to a series of books, *The One Hundred Cities of Italy.* Grazia invented another pseudonym, "G. Razia" for a number of poems which appeared in *Ultima Moda.* Her work was published in numerous magazines, and volumes of her fiction had been published by companies in Cagliari, Milan, and Rome. By now she had embarked on a prolific period as if her intellectual development had reached a point where nothing more could be absorbed without some outward expression. With normal channels of communication cut off by the hostility of her immediate surroundings, Grazia discovered that she had one patient, seemingly inexhaustible friend: the public. Into the silent ear of the blank page she continued to whisper.

Grazia's favorite season was summer: floral odors, festive holidays, and walks in the long sunset. But between the raging gossip in Nuoro about Grazia and the numerous Roman publications which carried her signature, Grazia was certain that Antonino Pau had heard about her literary activities. Of all the pettiness and criticism, Grazia feared only his. She dreaded the arrival of that summer, when Antonino, his head filled with university lectures, would return to Nuoro with his sarcastic wit, ready to tear into her little stories. She stood by her bedroom window, day after day, searching for a glimpse of Antonino. When he did not appear Grazia grew anxious, though she expected nothing from him, not the slightest sign of affection. No one, not even her sisters, suspected that she felt anything for him. Yet it was important that she face him not so much because she loved him, but because she needed to know if she was strong enough to withstand his ridicule.

One afternoon, Grazia and Beppa went to visit some girls they knew. These two sisters were Antonino's cousins and lived in the same family compound, but in a separate house. The four girls chatted while they had some coffee. Then they went for a stroll in the Pau vineyard from which there was a clear view of the sunset. The vineyard was enclosed by a long low stone wall. Beyond the wall, was a steep path that led from Nuoro, past the Deledda home, past the Pau compound and down to the valley. At the farthest corner of the vineyard, near Antonino's private "tower" sat the newly-arrived Antonino himself, absorbed in his newspaper. The summer sunset was pale yellow, like the gold-leaf background of a medieval icon. Astonished to see Antonino, Grazia stumbled over her own feet. Even Antonino's two cousins had not expected to see him there. They ran ahead of the two Deledda sisters and without even greeting him, began to beat their fists playfully on his knees. He shoved them aside, concerned about the crease in his trousers. He appeared ready to retreat with his newspaper into his private tower when he spotted Grazia. He jumped to his feet and greeted her with an elegant bow.

Grazia then tasted the exquisite, bittersweet pangs of unrequited love. Everything about him was luminous at that moment, a moment that would linger in her heart for a lifetime. The golden light of the sunset seemed to come from his eyes and from his dark face and his radiant hair. To the end of her life it was enough to think of him in order to feel a mysterious joy composed of light and agony.

Though Grazia had been bracing herself for weeks for the moment when she would have to defend her writing, Antonino expressed no curiosity about her stories. Instead, he inquired about Santus and promised to come by the house to visit him when her brother came home for the holiday. Grazia blushed, relieved not to have to discuss the "scandal" of her writing and delighted at the prospect of seeing Antonino again.

Antonino's two cousins stepped forward to pester him once more. Lennedda began poking and teasing him for the way he dressed. She even criticized his hair for being too shiny. "You put oil on it, like the women of Oliena," she accused him. "Who do you want to please in this primitive town? Here there are no young ladies!"

Grazia prayed that Antonino would reply to the saucy Lennedda in such a way that he might reveal his feelings. Instead, he just brushed his forehead with his hand, his fingernails reflecting the gold of the sunset through the dark strands of his hair. When Lennedda made a second insulting remark about his appearance, Grazia was mortified. She was delighted when Antonino swatted Lennedda's head with his rolled-up newspaper. This was not much of a deterrent to Lennedda. She reached up as if she was about to pull Antonino's hair. Quickly, Antonino seized his cousin, spun her around, and gave her a shove that made her topple over the vineyard wall down onto the path below. Shocked and bruised, Lennedda screamed as loudly as she could. Grazia was transfixed. She would have preferred never to have witnessed the incident, especially after having seen Antonino's cruel expression. Yet, in her heart she knew that had he done the same shameful thing to her, she would have been frightfully happy. Though Antonino seemed indifferent to her, Grazia suspected that Lennedda's "lesson" had been given in her honor. When Antonino nodded and walked away, oblivious to Lennedda's shrill screams, Grazia breathed a sigh of relief.

The summer passed leisurely. Santus seemed somewhat better, somewhat less addicted to drink. He would occasionally drink too much, but it did not seem to be as serious as before. Gionmario was at home, too, keeping rendezvous with Enza though Chiscedda and Totoni both knew what was going on. They could not interfere, however, because Totoni himself was quite ill. That spring he had suffered a stroke which left him unable to walk without help. He found it difficult even to speak. Confident that he would recover, the girls took care of him and Grazia read him the things she wrote.

At the end of the summer came the most splendid feast in

Nuoro, the feast of the Redeemer. The townspeople climbed up to Mount Orthobene where they camped outdoors for the nine days of the Novena. It was a period of prayer, meditation, song, and dance. It was not a solemn feast, for it celebrated the end of the harvest season. Enza and Chiscedda stayed behind to take care of Totoni. Grazia, Beppa and Nicolina accompanied Aunt Paolina whose servant drove the ox-cart which carried the bedding and utensils needed for the festival. The climb was tiring. After three hours they rested while the ox-cart crashed through the forest ahead of them. They rested near a pair of heavy stones, called the Tomb of the Giant. A layer of moss gave the stones the appearance of a sepulcher draped in velvet. According to legend, giants had once inhabited this mountain and they used to take turns guarding the entrance to the forest. When the last surviving giant died, the stone closed itself around him. Indeed, the forest itself seemed to enclose a heroic world, a world of titans too noble to do evil. Grazia touched the stone the way someone else might touch the headstone or reliquary of a saint. She yearned not only for purity of spirit, but also for a life different from the one which seemed to be her ineluctable fate.

When the climb resumed, Grazia felt that she had already started to escape the small world of Nuoro and that the ancient giants were helping her as she stumbled along the jagged footpath. The group stopped again to rest, this time beside a rare fountain of water, as pure and sparkling as diamonds. It sprang naturally from the earth, and it was surrounded by a small circle of stones. It was the source of a small stream that meandered through the forest. People often filled their jugs with this water, for it was said to have health-giving properties. The air was perfumed with the fragrance of mint. Grazia bent to drink from the sacred fountain. She looked at the reflection of her own eyes and saw that their light sprang from the depths, not from the sky. She knew, from that moment, that hers was a soul akin to the ancestral shepherds and poets of Barbagia.

After the long climb Grazia and the others arrived at the church of the Madonna of the Mountain. The chapel contained only a small altar, and its nave had been divided into rooms called *cumbessie.* During the festival, members of the wealthy families would sleep indoors while the other celebrants slept on the ground, beneath the stars. When Grazia's sisters first saw the earthen floors of their *cumbessia,* they cringed. Grazia, instead, welcomed the simplicity of the place as another element which would put her in touch with her remote past.

The smells of the humus and ferns, the crude cooking implements, the forest, the stones used as seats, all gave Grazia a sense of remote memories, as if she had dwelt there centuries ago. She watched the folk dances, and listened to the popular ballads. At night, when quiet descended, the rustle of the oak leaves in the forest soothed the sleepers with its organ-like sound. The moon appeared draped in silver. Grazia and her sisters were lulled by music that has no equal, for it was the music of childhood that resounds only once in life.

Besides the sweetness of the natural surroundings, the feeling of freedom, and even some time to herself in which to write, Grazia was gratified to discover that Antonino's family was staying in the *cumbessia* across the corridor. Antonino himself had not arrived, but like the other young men of Nuoro, he was expected. At night, young couples gathered to eat and to dance. They camped under the trees where they played games, sang, and courted. Some of the young men wooed their sweethearts with extemporaneous poetry songs and their manly charm. Watching these young shepherds and daughters of men like them, Grazia, at twenty, longed for companionship. She grew impatient to see Antonino once again, if only for a moment. Although she was tempted, she would not ask his relatives when he was expected, afraid that one of the sisters or cousins would guess her secret motive.

On one of the last days of the festival Antonino arrived, alone, by foot, with a staff in one hand and a straw hat in the other. Grazia, like some sort of forest elf, perched on a rock above the forest trail, and watched him as he approached, striking the ferns and bushes with his stick. He seemed thoroughly disgusted, as if the place were unworthy of him. Grazia could see that Antonino was out of place in the wild, as if he could enjoy only the artificial parks he found in Rome. Realizing how different Antonino was from herself, she felt all her love for him suddenly disappear. Nevertheless, his presence enhanced her enjoyment of the final moments of the celebration. In all, those days taught her the happiness available to the human soul when it is able to harmonize itself with nature. This was the most important discovery of her life, and formed the basis for the philosophy of all her mature work.

When Grazia returned to Nuoro, the big house seemed even more melancholic, decayed, damp. Totoni was slowly dying, and the funereal odor of chrysanthemums drifted from the gardens to the house. From her bedroom window Grazia could see the outline of Mount Orthobene where only days ago she had spent such happy hours. Now the wintry fog had all but obscured the peak.

The house seemed empty. Santus, stronger than he had been for a long time, had gone back to school. Andrea and his wild friends rode across the open fields. The four girls took turns caring for Totoni's increasing needs. Grazia, as if unwilling to face the terrible fact of Totoni's imminent death, submerged herself into the world of fantasy. Her whole perspective had changed. She seemed to write out of blind compulsion, or from a physical need, just as Andrea might streak across the countryside on horseback, or Enza might seek a secret lover, or Santus might obliterate reality with drink. Instead, Grazia invented her own escape, her own rendezvous in her writing. She created "Lara," a girl like herself, as the protagonist, in a world like her own, where the character's innocence and madness were those of Grazia herself. The story developed into *Fior di Sardegna* ("Flower of Sardinia"), into which she poured all her own sufferings.

"How could Lara refrain from dreaming, when she found herself alone for now, opposite the window, embroidering or knitting stockings? How not to dream in the deep winter night when the storm winds screamed outside and inside, the great fire crept into the blackened hall, and the servants narrated their legends of the mountains of Barbagia and Gallura, about women, fate, and horsemanship? How not to dream in the sunset of the emerald dusk of autumn or the blue summer nights when in the amber sky in the mysterious, perfumed distance, one could hear a sad, impassioned love song?

CHAPTER
SEVEN

Grazia completed *Fior di Sardegna* in July of 1891, before her twentieth birthday. Her motivation was a need to express her own vision to the world beyond the mountains of Barbagia. Moreover, she was determined to change the stereotype of her people. "I am very young and courageous," she wrote in a letter. "I adore art and my ideal is to raise up high the name of my homeland, so little known and denigrated in cultured lands."

Capitalizing on the new literary movement called "Verism," Grazia wrote to Magiorino Ferraris, an editor at the Perino publishing company in Rome. In her letter, she described *Fior di Sardegna* as being "so dramatic that it might be called sentimental, and perhaps even a bit Verist, if by *'verismo'* one means a portrait of life and men as they are, or, better yet, as I know them to be." She went on to explain that the book:

> faithfully portrays the life of the Sardinian "gentlefolk" whose life is completely different from that of [their counterparts] on the mainland. I faithfully describe our

original and bizarre traditions . . . the splendid unknown landscapes, . . . passions, types: in short, all the best that I thought would interest the reader, omitting the wild scenes and stories of blood which till now have made . . . our dear island thought of as a whirlpool of hatred and revenge.

After the letter was finished, and the carefully written pages of the manuscript were neatly arranged, Grazia took another sheet of paper and wrote her dedication. "To Contessa Elda di Montedoro." And who was this "contessa"? "She" was, in reality, a gentleman, named Epaminonda Provaglio, for it was deemed essential that readers of *Ultima Moda* believe that the magazine was under the direction of a fashionable woman. When Grazia first corresponded with *Ultima Moda* her letter was received by a man named Onorato Roux, an editor who soon transferred to the staff of another magazine. Provaglio, who took over his position, must have been self-conscious about his nom de plume, and clarified his identity to Grazia straight away. It was ironic that the same man who'd been obliged to adopt an aristocratic pseudonym had once been an ardent socialist in Mantua where he had been imprisoned with his associates for having published an antigovernment newspaper.

The company for which Provaglio worked, Perino, was virtually a publishing empire, and put out a number of popular magazines, books, and even some literary journals, each aimed at a different audience. Provaglio, therefore, was a valuable ally who acted as Grazia's story editor, mentor, friend, and even as interdepartmental agent. He himself was an author of over one hundred and fifty books, most published under pseudonyms. One of his novels, *Queen of the Fairies*, was given to Grazia as a present by none other than Antonino Pau who inscribed his name, the date — July 30, 1891 — and a note inside: "To Grazia Deledda, the eighteen-year-old Sardinian writer, dear to letters, the title of this book holds tribute of a fervid and constant admiration." (Grazia, twenty, and not eighteen, compensated for her inexperience as a writer by letting people believe she was younger than she really was — even Antonino was fooled!)

On the day that Grazia received Antonino's present, she wrote to the author himself, congratulating him, and indicating that she was about to send him the 200-page manuscript of *Fior di Sardegna*. She added, "If it would not be deemed inappropriate, I beg you to arrange the terms of the sale of the literary rights to my work with Signor Perino on my behalf." For two weeks she had been unable to mail the heavy manuscript, as she had no money for the stamps. Unlike her previous works — short stories, poems, and even the serialized novels — this large manuscript had to be sent as a package. If she told her family about the novel they would have kept her from sending it. One day, someone came to buy some of the olive oil stored in the Deledda cantina. Grazia waited on her and, putting some of the coins in her pocket, said nothing about the sale to her mother. She justified her theft by reminding herself of the way Andrea and Santus spent the family's money on wine. So she divided the money: half to the cash box, and half to "glory." After the manuscript was mailed, she went to Confession, saying that she had stolen some coins, but not admitting the motive, for she, unlike her family and the priests in Nuoro, did not regard writing as sinful.

It was not long before the publisher sent Grazia the galley sheets for her to correct any errors that may have crept in while setting the book in type. Grazia, however, had no idea what they were and put them aside. Soon, a letter arrived from the editor, who demanded that she make the corrections immediately and return the galley sheets. Reluctantly Grazia set about correcting the many typographical errors. In Nuoro, Italian was a foreign, purely literary language. She struggled with the corrections, making them a novel way, in between the printed lines just above the words so that the pages seemed to be covered with savage flowerings of scribbles, a tangle that must have terrorized the poor typesetter destined to unravel it.

Grazia sold more oil and pocketed the profits in her apron so that she could mail the galley sheets back to Rome. No sooner had that been accomplished when a letter from the publisher asked her to send a photograph for the frontispiece of the book. Grazia wanted a romantic picture taken of herself with her hair loose, wearing her new violet dress with a silver pin at the neckline. The picture came out grim. She looked angry, wild, disdainful. She did not want to be depicted in this way, for she knew that beneath her adolescent awkwardness there was someone beautiful and refined. Again, more half-liters of oil and wine were omitted from the family's balance sheets, and the coins reserved for a new photograph.

The second one, made sometime in August, showed a proper Victorian young lady. Grazia's head emerged from a broad fan made of black ostrich feathers which the young writer had spread artfully across her minuscule bosom. She credited the success of the photograph to the romantic notions of the photographer, who imagined that the picture was destined for a beau. In a sense he was right, for Grazia regarded the public as her first, distant lover, who was rich and kind, and powerful. She foresaw that *Fior di Sardegna*'s readers would be as young as she, and therefore close to her own soul and to her own fantasies.

Fior di Sardegna was published toward the end of February 1892. Grazia received a disappointing message: in lieu of royalties, she was being sent one hundred copies of her book. Though shaken by the news, Grazia wrote to Provaglio, who arranged the terms of the sale with his Perino colleagues. The value of the books did not even equal the price of the oil and wine she had stolen in order to buy her stamps but Grazia managed to retain her sense of humor. "I received a notice today from Macomer that my hundred copies have arrived at the train station there . . ." she wrote, "they are going to forward them to me, here, so that I can bestow [the books] as gifts to my friends, to friends of friends, to enemies, to enemies of enemies . . ." However she couldn't even give many of the books away. Signor Carlino wouldn't have them in his bookstore, nor would another relative, a barber, allow her to display them in his shop. Once again, Nuoro was in a uproar over Grazia.

But, *Fior di Sardegna* did bring letters from the public. For the first time Grazia was requested to explain why she decided to write. "I write," she explained to an admirer by the name of Luppini, "because I dream of fame, which, I know intuitively I shall never achieve. Thus, I wander through life here in Sardinia which is madness, tracing and consuming my youth before a golden dream which I know to be a mirage and which I must pursue, for, without it I would die of boredom." To Luppini's advice that she come to Rome, she replied, "I forsee that one day I must leave my rocky island, and this,

110

indeed is one of my most ardent desires; but for now, this is fine . . . The Sardinian life is less monotonous and sad than you perhaps imagine. No, indeed, life is sweeter here than any artist would desire." This letter was sent to Provaglio for forwarding to the young poet Luppini. Apparently, the "contessa" decided that this was not prudent, for the letter remained tucked away inside his desk drawer. Grazia was confused by Luppini's apparent discourtesy. She had even dedicated a children's story, "Giaffah" to him when it was published in *Paradiso dei Bambini* in six parts between May and June. In mid-June, Grazia mentioned in a letter to Provaglio that Luppini had not replied to her letter.

When Grazia received no reply, either from Luppini or from Provaglio, she began to suspect that something was wrong. She received a letter in late July from Provaglio informing her that his youngest son, Ciro, had died. "How sad, how sad, I am. My poor *babbo* is quite ill, more than ever, and it should not be long before he will join your Ciro. The thought of death for my father weighs down on my mind constantly and I feel the gloomy presentiment of mourning, imminent and close by. Thus, the announcement of someone else's mourning gives me cold shivers . . . Oh, poor little one! But no, he is not poor! The only comfort which I could give you is to tell you that it is perhaps better that he is dead. Why live, when life is so sad and so desolate? Look, if it is true that there is an afterlife, your little one has gone there, to heaven, where he will not suffer, where he will never despair. Strange comfort, mine! But I do not know how to express . . . exactly how my spirit feels."

Provaglio, the ex-socialist, had not allowed any of his children to be baptized. Under pressure from his family,

111

however, he had yielded. Grazia was to have been the godmother of his middle son, Mario. A week after the death of the infant, Ciro, the prospective *commare* received another shock when a second death notice arrived from Provaglio, indicating that Mario had fallen into a lake and drowned. Grazia suffered, knowing what terrible grief Provaglio and his wife had to endure, superstitiously apprehensive that death would strike once again. She wrote a second letter of condolence, as unconventional as the first. "You cannot imagine how I loved your Mario. I dreamed God knows what things on his account, certain that one day or another I would see him. And instead! But it is useless to rebel against fate . . . You and your wife shall forget . . . the sad present, and perhaps someday you shall bless death for having taken your babies before they came to suffer their own sorrow. Meager and pessimistic comfort, mine, isn't it? But see, we Sards almost never cry for dead babies — instead many, on this island cry at the birth of a new creature thinking of the sad events of life . . . My poor *babbo* has revived and I hope that for now the sad god does not come to disrupt my tranquil and silent household . . . Remaining between us is the bond, which in Sardinia, is considered the most sacred that can exist between two friends."

Grazia's intimacy with Provaglio was not unique. Her youth, her skill as a writer, and her proud sincerity had impressed everyone to whom she wrote. Without study, and without ever having left what she termed her "savage niche," Grazia had launched herself on her own career. When she was nineteen she had informed the director of the Perino publishing company, "I need a guide, but only for about another year. I feel — and I say this without false modesty, confident I will not be misunderstood — that I have no fear of anything or anyone. I am less than twenty. By thirty, I wish to have reached my scope, that is to create, by myself alone, a literature completely and exclusively Sardinian."

She also corresponded with authors, editors, critics, and journalists. One was count Angelo de Gubernatis, a brillant linguist and scholar who had begun to collect regional folklore from the rural areas of Italy. Grazia contributed to his journal, *Natura ed Arte.* Another was Onorato Roux, the man who had preceded Epaminonda Provaglio as the "contessa" and who, after editing two children's magazines, *Paradiso dei Bambini* (Paradise of the Little Ones) and *Il Giornaletto dei ragazzi* (Children's Journal), both of which published Grazia's work, was to become a famous literary critic. Another man to whom she wrote was the critic Cesari, whose book *Vigliaccherie femminili* (Feminine Cowardice) she reviewed in the June 12, 1892 issue of *Vita Sarda*, a Sardinian newspaper, but she dropped him after he gave one of *her* stories a bad review. Grazia also admired a writer and critic named Boccafurni, who had created a scandal in Italy when he left the priesthood and married. She dedicated stories to these and other men as well. But none of these men intrigued her as much as Stanis Manca, who was not only the drama critic for the *Tribuna* of Rome, but, as the Duke of Asinara's son, was a Sardinian nobleman to boot.

Their correspondence began when Manca wrote to Grazia to express his admiration of *Fior di Sardegna*. A fellow Sardinian, he was deeply impressed by her descriptions and by her use of the Sardinian setting to enhance the story. So sincere was Stanis's letter that Grazia sensed she had finally found someone who, by virtue of language, blood, and literary

113

interests, could truly understand her. Since he was a journalist, his admiration was a distinction. Grazia replied quickly and enclosed five of her poems, ones she had written at sixteen and seventeen. He appreciated her gift but he could not resist the desire to criticize her excessive fantasy. Grazia, however, defended herself in her next letter. "A poet without fantasy shouldn't compose verse!" In her next letter to Stanis Manca, in August, Grazia explained her motivation in writing.

> I do not dream of glory out of vanity or egoism, but because I love my homeland intensely and I dream one day to be able . . . to tell, completely, the life and passions of my people, . . . so scorned and neglected, and, as a result, most miserable in their . . . primitive ignorance. . . . One could say that glory is a frightening thing. One could smile at the temerity of my foolish fixation, to think that it is beyond my ability to assert myself, to think I can never attain my goal, that it is not expected from a poor, humble girl, with neither education nor sponsor, to resurrect the name of a land. One laughs at all this, just as I myself laugh in my moments of lucidity . . . I am still quite young, and therefore, I still have illusions which will vanish with experience.

In Stanis' reply he indicated that he hoped to be able to call on Grazia when he visited his family in Sardinia. Grazia promptly replied that she would be happy to receive him, adding sarcastically that, while her house was too humble for the son of an old and aristocratic Sardinian family, it would probably not bother a newspaperman. She continued, in a more serious vein, to explain herself to him, sensing that his visit would be a momentous occasion in her life. Grazia was excited by the prospect of meeting someone almost her age, someone who was so interested in her that he was willing to travel all the way from Rome to see her. In her last letter to Stanis before his departure, Grazia confessed that while she was subject to all the same passions, all the same defects and dreams of any other young person, what set her apart was her grand dream — a dream so overpowering that it obscured everything else. It was a dream she regretted, for it played tricks on her, and never left her in peace. "It is a mad, crazy, unfounded dream which God must have given me in a moment of wicked humor!" she complained, "It is the dream of Glory: a foolish dream for a mere woman, and even more for one like me who is a nobody . . . It is too late to laugh at this strange madness. Seeing the monotony and the futility of my life, I plunge headlong upon a sea of visions."

Stanis Manca traveled by ship across the rough sea that separates Sardinia from Rome, and journeyed on horseback through steep, wild, almost barren terrain to reach Nuoro. It was a festive day for Grazia, and a day of great humiliation as well, for the refinement of a man such as Manca made everything around him seem crude and battered. The De-ledda home, already in half-mourning for the impending death of Totoni, seemed old and stifling. She was embarrassed by her neighbors and even her own sisters who gaped at the sight of the tall, blond, green-eyed aristocrat. Even Grazia had to admit, however, that she was not physically attracted to him, yet it was a time in her life when she was predisposed to fall in love, and so she did, though she herself never quite understood why.

Grazia, dressed in her finest, received him in the office that Totoni had used for his business before he became ill. She was dismayed to see that a layer of dust clung to the books and ledgers, and that everything seemed disorganized and about to fall apart. They spoke and shared the strong Sardinian coffee that Grazia's sisters served.

During their two hours together Stanis was favorably impressed with Grazia, though she could never be more than a friend to him. The interview was published in a September issue of the *Tribuna* of Rome. Manca had been astonished to find such a clever young woman in Nuoro. In his interview he remarked on "the vivacious geniality of our small George Sand. How modern is her culture, and how many innovative ideas are in her mind . . ."

> To see her, so tiny, with her large, black, pensive eyes, like the heroines of her stories, pale with an aristocratic pallor, nervous, with a smile both gentle and teasing, dressed elegantly in black, with the blackest of hair . . . to tell the truth, she gave me a strange and bizarre impression that I was not dealing with a girl from Sardinia . . . Instead, she seemed to be like one of those dainty, exotic figurines which one sees while walking past the shop windows along the via Caracciolo in Naples.

In his article Stanis had called her "a dainty figurine," which indicated to Grazia that he, too, was in love. She wrote to him proclaiming her lasting friendship. Her letters to Stanis were direct and sincere. She told him of her dreams and her struggles. As a fellow Sardinian he understood the prejudices that worked against her. She even described her working habits to him, "I am studying constantly the strange conversations of our workers (which make me laugh); my neighbors' gossip; the small love stories of the common people; the cruel tales, so full of passion and blood that they don't seem real. But I feel unable to depict my people yet. I will do it later on . . . I confess to you that I haven't acquired the power to treat this harsh subject yet . . . I hesitate so that my pen can age, and that the precision of my mind can become more acute in order to enable me to write a novel of the people."

Early in January 1892, Stanis informed Grazia that one of the Sardinian papers had requested permission to reprint his interview with her. This news flattered her and she wrote back inquiring if he would be willing to mention her book, *Fior di Sardegna*, in one of his columns. Curiously, she decided to add a kind of warning, ". . . I hope you will not be scandalized if, in my story, [the heroine] has nocturnal rendezvous with her lover — because I have observed that you are a bit of a Quaker on this point. You wouldn't do me the horrible wrong, so much in vogue in Sardinia, of believing that beneath the guise of my heroine I have hidden myself. No, you mustn't do me this wrong because you know me well enough."

Despite this disclaimer, Grazia's friend Stanis would not have been wrong had he suspected that his little "figurine" was lying, for not only was Grazia in love with him, but she was passionately in love with a schoolteacher who lived in Nuoro as well! Andrea Pirodda was the opposite of Manca: dark, fine-boned, and earthy. When the intelligent, appealing Andrea ambitiously courted Grazia she felt tremendous physical attraction for him.

But Grazia knew from the precedent of Gionmario that her parents were not romantic fools. With this in mind she kept Andrea Pirodda a secret from her family while at the same time dreaming about Stanis Manca. Of all the men she knew, only Stanis could take her away from the monotony of Sardinia. He knew everyone in the theatrical and artistic world of Rome. What was more, he continued to answer her letters and he had even stated his esteem publicly, having called her his "small, great friend." His letters were so courteous that one might interpret them as letters of courtship. One day, Grazia's brother, Andrea managed to intercept and read one and even he seemed pleased about it. Finally, here was someone good enough for his little sister. *Why not marry the blond giant*, Grazia thought, while within her a terrible struggle began to grow: two lovers as different as night and day and indecision which to choose. If she wanted fame and fortune, Stanis was the one. But if she wanted tenderness and passion and true love, Andrea Pirodda would have been her only choice.

Andrea Pirodda was also Sardinian, having been born in 1868 in the town of Aggius in the northern part of the island. He had come to Nuoro to teach elementary school, but he had not completed his education. His family was poor, hardly any better off than the coal miners in their district. Pirodda was a handsome, seductive young man who had loved Grazia from afar. Shortly before she was to meet Stanis Manca, Grazia finally became aware of Pirodda's interest. In mid-August she wrote a poem about her admirer: "I loved you because you were alone and sad . . . you have filled the empty void which strangles me . . . I am re-born!"

Grazia enjoyed the intrigue of her first real romance. She would stand near her high bedroom window and wait for Pirodda to pass below on his way home from school: "Did you see me smile when you passed?" she wrote in a note smuggled to him inside a borrowed book. "I did it but no one saw me."

In another smuggled letter she wrote, "Every Sunday morning I go to Mass at the Church of the Rosary; I will sit in front of you there." How complicated all this was. They were alone only at night when Grazia could creep out into the garden to be with him. At twenty-one, Grazia was understandably anxious to taste all the pleasures of love. But under the circumstances, with such a dubious future, frustration seems to have intensified the physical passion between the two lovers. "Our lips shall unite in the first kiss of our fervid love . . ." she wrote him. "I shall put my arms around your neck, strongly, strongly, and I shall kiss you so ardently, so intensely that I may swoon. Oh, when, when shall I be able to kiss you like that, and to show you with my eyes, with my kiss, all my love, dear, adored one?"

Despite her intense feelings, in time Grazia began to see Andrea's faults. She even began to suspect that he was interested in her because her family owned a great deal of property. Finally, she recognized that Andrea was not her intellectual equal. He was too vain to accept Grazia's clear superiority in the area of writing. Though she was ready to challenge her family for the right to marry him, Grazia's judgment remained clear and objective. Her letters to her confidant Epidamonda Provaglio reveal that she was divided between her accurate estimation of Andrea's literary mediocrity and her urgent desire for him. Almost as soon as she fell in love with him, she knew that to accept him as a husband would require the sacrifice of her own dreams. Still under the spell of first love, Grazia announced to the "contessa": "I am beloved. He is a young, good, brave, and handsome man who adores me . . . My dream was to marry myself to someone who would take me far from here, to a land of culture and intelligence. To accept this one, I run the risk of staying here forever."

By October Grazia had had time to read Andrea's literary efforts. She was a harsh critic and she reported to Provaglio that she had advised Andrea, "one needs to rise up a bit higher to become the husband of a writer, dear." Pirodda began to display some other irritating habits. One was to send his work to the magazines that published Grazia's stories. When he went to Rome he made contact with her editor Provaglio, and introduced himself as Grazia's cousin. While he may have advised her beforehand, clearly Andrea was using Grazia to advance himself.

Andrea Deledda, returning home one night, discovered Pirodda serenading Grazia, and chased him away. The next day Grazia was confronted by her brother, who told her to stop seeing Pirodda. He was so incensed that he beat her and later reported Grazia's behavior to their parents.

In January, Grazia confided to Provaglio that in view of her family's objections, her future with Pirodda seemed unpromising. The family compared him to Stanis Manca and demonstrated the miserable life she would have to lead with a husband as poor as Pirodda. "Maybe they are right," she conceded. "I don't know . . . I hope and despair in the future." In the spring things looked a little more promising. "My idyll continues," she informed the "contessa," "the sky has turned blue and my hopes are the same." After a whole year of torment, Grazia was caught in the dilemma of loving two men, both desirable and yet each unsuitable in his own way. Pirodda was at hand, and physically attractive but poor. Manca was in Rome, only platonically attractive and rich — far too rich.

Andrea Pirodda, realizing the Deledda family opposition, tried to make Grazia promise to marry him before he took a new post near Sassari. By then, Grazia knew that marriage either to Pirodda or to Manca was impossible, and she suffered terribly. "I have lost a count for a suitor," she lamented to Provaglio.

> I have decided to love a poor teacher who is nothing but a mediocre artist and for this reason tries to write and publish almost in my footsteps. But, what do you want? I am happy and fiery in my love because Andrea, my beloved Andrea, is young, better, and more virtuous than one can say. I have seen in his personality no trace of materialism. I have seen his soul . . . and I would love him merely because I found his spirit the best, most loyal, most honest, and straightest in the world. Don't think I exaggerate or that love has blinded me . . . Now, understand that my family opposes our matrimony. But in the coming year or at most two, he will take his diploma and a post as a professor — it is the lack of a degree that my family minds — and then we can get married. In any case, I do not expect, privately, a brilliant future [for him], but that doesn't bother me. My life shall be short, ten years at most, and I wish to enjoy it spiritually in that happiness that wealth does not give. Today Andrea departed . . . I am very sad and I fall into the cold sea of desperation.

During the separation, Andrea found a job teaching in the harshest, poorest place in Sardinia, Buggeru. He taught coal miners' children soon destined for the mines themselves after the minimum four years of school were over. This made

Grazia's anguish even worse. To be poor was one thing, but to live in a place so ugly, so utterly impoverished, to witness the exploitation and near-slavery of the miners was something she could never bear.

Each day Grazia worked on her stories, and she began another novel. But even these things could not distract her from the constant anxiety about Pirodda. "Each day that passes increases the obstacles and the distance between him and me," she confided to Provaglio. "He is good and upright, but he is too poor, too low to approach me, or better, to arrive at the point at which my people could love him." She seemed desperate.

> Sometimes I am tempted to get married simply to change my existence, but I think I would repent two hours afterward, so I drop the idea. And then there is Andrea, that poor Andrea, who would die of pain . . . The first of August I had a grand suitor, an owner of villages, rich, young, and ugly. You know, I was about to accept him? Then I feel sick, and in the sad sleepiness of my fever I thought better about what I was doing, and then I bade him good-bye . . . It would be better to die.

Nevertheless, unable to break completely from Andrea, Grazia continued to pledge her fidelity to him in her letters, "I tell you, you must discard the idea of sacrificing yourself for me! Know well: if you . . . wish to leave me, just leave me. I will not die perhaps because solitude [has made me] resistant to blows of this type. I would not die, no, and maybe I could even arrive at that luminous stage to which I believe I am destined. But life will be morally broken, everything would be dead." She reassured her unfortunate lover by saying, "Have pity on me and say no more that I might one day despise you!"

Ironically, Grazia was already convinced that all their lovers' pledges would, in the end, be broken. "He could become a most outstanding professor, but you know how? Between five, to eight or even ten years," she lamented to Provaglio.

And I, in all that time, might well waste my life in silence and waiting, merely to die before he could attain the rank demanded by my family, and which appeals even to my reason . . . He is not an artist. He hasn't the power necessary to succeed . . . He will never be anything but a poor teacher. [My family] wishes another, because I, in my career, need to be sustained by a strong man. I need support, help, counsel and even relative comforts . . . My family wishes that I break off this relationship, and I must break it off . . . I suffer, suffer, suffer, and my heart breaks, but I must make the sacrifice . . . My brother insists and my mother prays each day that I end this sad idyll which makes me suffer and makes me ill.

During all of the emotional turmoil within Grazia's heart, another terrible sorrow occurred. Her beloved father Totoni died. At his death the family went into deep mourning. Grazia felt lost, for in his last months she had grown closer than ever. Yet, with his death it seemed to Grazia that Totoni's spirit would remain always within her, to protect her from danger and guide her. Grazia detested the artifice of mourning. What she felt in her heart was enough. She submitted, but all the while, she resented the hypocrisy social convention imposed. She and her sisters were very sad. Their young lives seemed crushed under the monotony of the mourning. The house was darkened, the windows were shuttered, and no one could go near the glass to look out. This was the worst for Grazia, not to be able even to look at the countryside. For two of three months the women all had to stay shut up inside the house and after that they could make only short trips to church or visits to relatives. They were forbidden from shopping or going for a stroll in town. Luckily they were permitted to walk in the fields where Grazia was happiest. They were not allowed to attend festivals or celebrations and they had to wear solemn faces and to dress in black at all times. This enforced mourning lasted for a long time — for five years for Chiscedda, the widow, but Grazia decided to end the hypocrisy after two, for she felt the artificiality, combined with her true sorrow, was going to kill her.

Grazia prayed, and prayed some more. She prayed partly for the dead, but primarily for the living, for she could tell that the rest of the family was demoralized, shaken like dry grass in the shadow of a lightning-felled oak. From the day Totoni died in November of 1892, the Deledda family seemed to fall apart. Grazia went about her household chores and her reading and she wrote to pass the time, to kill the monotony. In her writing she had found her true existence.

CHAPTER
EIGHT

The next eight years of Grazia Deledda's life were filled with anxiety, sorrow, and tragedy, even though there were moments of glory. She had to share the responsibilities of the household, though the cheerful company of Beppa and Nicolina did little to relieve the monotony. The melancholic Chiscedda had to deal with four marriageable daughters and two irresponsible sons. Enza complained constantly that Grazia did nothing but stay in her room, read and write, and that she never helped out with the housework.

The family had suffered more than just the loss of a beloved husband and father. Totoni's death completely altered the family's social status in the eyes of the townspeople of Nuoro. Everything that Grazia had written was now openly ridiculed and Chiscedda was accused of being a negligent mother. People gossiped about the girls and rumors abounded about their "flirtatious" behavior.

Chiscedda did not know what to do when she first heard the rumor that an illegitimate baby, born to a beautiful peasant girl, had been fathered by Andrea. But by then just about everything was being blamed on him. Chiscedda lost sleep,

terrified that Andrea would waste away all the family income
— now fully in his hands — and that the tax-collector,
Antonino Pau's father, would come to appropriate the house
and all the property. Fortunately, Chiscedda had inherited
some property at the death of her mother, and she counted on
that as security against Andrea's flagrant irresponsibility.

Santus, away at school during Totoni's final months of
agony, suffered even more than the other children, for he was
the eldest. Fear of disgracing his father, combined with his
determination to finish medical school, had kept Santus going.
When Totoni died, Santus was in the middle of his third year.
He managed to complete the year and he came back to Nuoro
for his summer holiday. People in his hometown were
scandalized by his chronic drunkenness, though it harmed no
one but himself. When he was sober, however, instead of
studying, he made toys for the neighborhood children, as if he
were reverting to the personality of "Su Santaiu" the grandfather for whom he had been named. Santus spent that last
summer holiday in a sort of trance. For some, the death of a
father would have revived a sense of responsibility, but
Totoni's death seemed to make the dreamer more and more
passive each day. When it came time for Santus to leave
Nuoro for his final year of medical studies, however, he seemed
to have pulled himself together. On the day of departure the
family had a feast: boiled octopus, wild boar ham, boiled
blackbirds, a cheese soup, dumplings with tomato sauce, three
different kinds of bread, stuffed chicken, beans, cabbage,
cheeses, white grapes, sweet cakes, almond candies, and strong
coffee. Wine was on the table for the guests, but Santus,
seemingly ambitious, sober, and happy, declined to drink it.
Andrea and the girls went to the train station to wave

good-bye while Chiscedda secretly went to the church to pray. She had such confidence in Santus that she had given him a small cache of coins that she had accumulated bit by bit for emergencies. Everyone returned to the house happy and in good spirits. Andrea bragged that when Santus next returned they would have to call him "doctor." Upstairs, the windows of Santus's bedroom were flung open as if the room were being aired following someone's recovery from a long illness. Finally, after a seemingly endless period of sorrow and mourning, Chiscedda was smiling and partaking in the activities and conversations of her daughters.

Six months after Santus had departed and only a few months before graduation, the silence of midnight was shattered by someone knocking over and over and over at the heavy front door. It was a sound so morbid and so frightening that Grazia never forgot it. To her it was a noise more terrifying than the fire-bell, the sound of the drum that heralds disaster, a sound made by the beating heart, or by the drummer who walks before the coffin in a Sardinian funeral procession.

Nanna went to the door, frightened that it might be a bandit, or even a man of *zusisstia* that is, a police officer, pursuing someone. *Perhaps it was a ghost, a dead man who passes in the street and knocks at the door to warn the living that Hell awaits them too*, she thought. Nanna opened the door. It was worse. Far worse. It was a living corpse who announced hell, yes, but the one before death, the living death. It was Santus, his blue eyes forever clouded, his body limp. He was unable to talk, unable to make sense out of what people were saying. He had squandered all his money and had now returned, half-mad, to that already sad house, never to leave again.

The repercussions were immediate. The entire town sprang upon the tragic incident as if waiting, hoping for such a sad disgrace to befall the powerful Deledda family. The severest judgments came from people who had just as much to hide, if not more. The two old spinsters, Chiscedda's cousins, with whom Sebastiano lived, were the worst. These were the same illiterate cousins who had burnt the issue of *Ultima Moda* in which Grazia's first story appeared. They spent most of their time in church or with their neighbors, trading gossip and rumors which they in turn would eagerly pass along to the person being maligned. Whenever they visited the Deledda home they sat as stiff as a pair of mummies. They did not seem to know how to talk without making cruel, cutting remarks, and they found fault with everything, even when life was going along well. They constantly criticized Chiscedda for allowing her daughters to wear new dresses or to put ribbons in their hair when they were supposed to be in mourning for their father.

The very morning after Santus returned, these two spinsters came to the house and badgered Chiscedda to the point that she began to weep. Having succeeded in humiliating the already unstable Chiscedda, they continued to make vicious attacks against her. The Deledda sisters hung by the door, out of sight, dismayed and confused because they thought Santus could be helped, though apparently their mother did not. As if the first diatribe was not enough, the spinsters' next subject was Enza, whose "secret" love for Gionmario Mesina was, by now, unofficially tolerated by the family. These two barren harpies who had never experienced love, regarded the pathetic romance of the two young people as something tragic and horrible, and by making innuendoes about Paolo and Francesca and other doomed adulterous lovers, suggested that Enza was a wild, immoral young woman.

Chiscedda could not hold back her tears. She had been hurt by the things said about her daughter. Her own hostility toward Gionmario had diminished and she had come to realize that an organized and energetic young man would have strengthened the family under recent circumstances. She was unable to rebuke the women's vicious accusations and to Enza, who was, of course, eavesdropping, her silence seemed like agreement. The hypersensitive girl screamed and crashed to the floor in a seizure. Seeing this, Chiscedda rose and chased the two wicked women out of the house and went to console Enza. Finally the children realized that Chiscedda, though melancholic, withdrawn, and even somewhat intimidated by the better-educated members of her family, regarded all of them, including Santus — or rather, him more than the others — as delicate creatures whom the Lord permitted to grow and to become wise. Though she had always appeared passive and solemn, she loved her children intensely, and she knew intuitively that each of them suffered from the impoverished social environment of Nuoro.

The eviction of the two aunts only intensified gossip. Knowing that these women had destroyed any chance of her marrying another man, Enza's family officially recognized Gionmario as her fiancé. They were married in the summer of 1893, immediately following Gionmario's graduation from law school. Since the family was still in mourning, the wedding was modest and dreary, with none of the traditional ingredients of Sardinian nuptials: laughter, joy, dancing, music, the recitation of poetry, and all the traditional feasts and rituals.

From the beginning, Enza and Gionmario were unhappy.

Neither was stable, and the marriage foundered because of their immaturity. In early November, Grazia confided to the folklorist and scholar Angelo de Gubernatis (to whom Grazia had sent a number of articles on the customs and songs of Barbagia) that things were not going well: "My family is in complete discord. After their little honeymoon my sister and her husband came to live with us. Now, my brother [Andrea] and my brother-in-law have been arguing over a question of money. My sister and her husband, still almost children, like myself, have left without even saying good-bye."

The couple stayed for a while in the gloomy home of Gionmario's parents. Realizing, however, that the marriage would disintegrate there, Chiscedda offered them the use of the large old house she had inherited from her parents. It had a steep staircase and huge rooms with wooden floors, small windows, and whitewashed walls. No one had occupied it since Chiscedda's mother had died, a few years earlier, and it needed a great deal of scrubbing and repairs in addition to routine housecleaning. Even with the help of a part-time maid, Enza soon wore herself out trying to make the house livable. This exhaustion, combined with her neurotic tendencies and Gionmario's intense almost paranoid stubbornness, strained the relationship to its limit. Gionmario was lucky enough to find a post as a clerk in a lawyer's office. This apprenticeship, however, would last two or three years during which he would receive no salary. Since his own parents could give him very little help, Gionmario was obliged to depend on his in-laws and the small income from his wife's inheritance.

After three years Enza's depression and physical exhaustion exasperated Gionmario. Without even trying to work out an understanding, they fought constantly. Ironically, as Gionmario's apprenticeship grew to an end, the explosions between them became more and more furious. A pattern of accusation and self-deception began. Gionmario began to reproach Enza for having insisted upon getting married too soon. She replied that he had tricked her into loving him so that he would get her father's money. The arguments were painful and violent, and their brief reconciliations never came to grips with the real problems between them. Gionmario's "solution" was to stay away from the house as much as possible.

One December morning, two days after Christmas, Enza's maid came running to the Deledda house. She was frightened out of her wits, stammering that she had found her mistress lying lifeless on her bed. The maid had managed to revive Enza momentarily, but she sensed Enza's condition was serious. Chiscedda was suffering from a kidney disorder, so the three Deledda sisters decided not to alarm her. Instead, Grazia ran to her sister's house praying that the maid had mistaken one of Enza's epileptic seizures for something worse.

When she arrived at the house, Grazia found Enza lying on the bed. She was calm and pale, with fear in her eyes, unable to speak or move. Grazia smelled an unfamiliar and repulsive odor. She was almost overcome by fright and had to force herself to pull back the sheets and clothing which covered her sister. She discovered that Enza was lying in a black pool of her own blood. The maid fetched the doctor. He examined the semiconscious Enza, and determined that she had suffered a miscarriage. Both he and Grazia did what they could, but it was too late. The maid was sent out again for Gionmario, but before the young husband could get to the house, Enza died.

This was, perhaps, the most terrible event of Grazia's life. Though fascinated by stories of passion and revenge, Grazia had been sheltered from true violence. Now, she was confronted with tragic reality: the brutal death of a beautiful sister. Enza was dead — without pain, without consciousness, so pale and beautiful, her corpse looked like an exact portrait carved out of white marble.

Acting on impulse, Grazia performed the mortician's tasks, closing Enza's big eyes, washing the sweat and blood from her body, and carrying her to a small couch in the sitting room next to the bedroom. She perfumed Enza, combed her chestnut hair, and arranged it around her diaphanous face. Then Grazia dressed Enza in her modest wedding gown and put the satin wedding shoes on her feet.

All of this horrified Grazia, but somehow her patience, stamina, and family loyalty kept her from collapsing. She was determined to shield her mother and the rest from the malicious curiosity of those who would have congratulated themselves on the accuracy of their earlier predictions. Grazia herself did not quite understand how she withstood the tragedy. An intoxication of pain, disillusion, and fear left Grazia — like all violent intoxications — with a trace of bitterness or terror, which she buried at the bottom of her heart, like an unintended sin.

Again there was mourning and sorrow, and the windows were shuttered. Grazia continued to write, dreaming, praying for a way to escape to a better life. She was not alone in this ambition. Yet, it was an aspiration that had already proved to be dangerous, having already cost Santus his sanity and Enza her life. The next victim of the dream was to be Andrea who had been caught showing off for his drunken friends by stealing chickens.

Andrea's search for a better, more adventurous life ended

abruptly. He was arrested and brought before a judge who saw before him the son of a former mayor, a prosperous young man, no longer the age when adolescent rebelliousness might be tolerated. To set an example, Andrea received a ten year sentence at the prison at Cagliari.

With an ailing mother who suffered from severe depression, one half-mad brother, and the other brother in jail, Grazia became the head of the household. She managed everything, taking over Andrea's duties such as bookkeeping and correspondence, paying bills, and the supervision of the oil press. The press was an important aspect of the family income. Olive growers from the entire zone would bring their wagonloads of olives to the Deledda press. After the total quantity was recorded, their olives would be pressed and an equivalent amount of oil would be returned, minus a certain proportion that was left as payment. The Deleddas sold this oil from their home. Grazia was responsible for the records and she occupied the small dusty office in one part of the press where she could observe, unseen, the activities of the workers and clients. Those who gathered there had nothing to do but to wait for their oil and to exchange gossip. Grazia could see that there were many people worse off than either of her brothers.

Grazia was aware of theories popular at that time concerning racially determined levels of intelligence. Proponents of the theory used cranial measurements to substantiate their belief in white supremacy. In addition to blacks, ethnic minorities thought to be culturally inferior to the dominant racial group were also found to be lacking in "thinking capacity" according to these measurements. The Sardinians fit perfectly into this category: conditions on the island were the most primitive in Europe, their culture was completely alien from mainlanders, and they were physically diminutive with proportionately small skulls. The fallacious theory remained undisputed for decades, during which time the failures of the dominant social systems were attributed to the victims, who were also tricked into accepting the status quo.

Two visiting anthropologists who advocated this theory came to Nuoro to examine human skulls. Grazia was attracted to their theories because, if true, they justified Andrea's, Santus's, and Enza's failures as well as the poverty, disease, and abuse suffered by most of the Sardinian people. However, brought up in a Catholic environment — even one that clung to superstitious beliefs in "Fate" — Grazia had doubts. She used the olive press like a scientist in a laboratory. Day and night, the huge fire burned beneath the cauldron of boiling water used to sterilize the sacks that filtered the oil. Around that blaze huddled the downtrodden poor of Barbagia. Santus spent most of his time there, as well, and Grazia was on her guard against someone trying to take advantage of him. She soon observed, however, that despite his confused state of mind, he was able to discern true friends from false. This collection of human wrecks shared wine and food, favorite arias and folksongs, and they toasted one another's health and narrated the sad twists of "fate" that had brought them down.

Upon the advice of her mentors, Provaglio and Angelo de Gubernatis, the sociolinguist, Grazia had been writing stories about the poor of her district since September 1892. She regarded these stories as "socialistic" for they dealt with poverty, suffering, and moral vindication. In the olive press, she began her first socialistic novel, *La via del male* ("The Way of Evil") which she dedicated, ironically, to the visiting anthropologists Niceforo and Orano. Almost as soon as this work was completed, she began a second socialistic novel, *Anime oneste* ("Honest Souls") and sent it to Treves, a publisher who was quick to put it into print. *La via del male* languished on an editor's desk at a different publisher for months, to Grazia's consternation, before being rejected. Finally, Treves of Milan published it in 1896, nearly a year after *Anime oneste*, and with these two books began Grazia's lifelong association with one of the finest publishers in Italy. The books took Italy by storm. Even the critics were astonished, for her earlier work had been so radically different. Grazia became an overnight success.

Being a *cause célèbre* at twenty-five was not everything Grazia had hoped it would be. She still had to cope with family problems, the business, and her other obligations. At about this time she was offered the position as headmistress of a newly built kindergarten in Nuoro. She was hoping to accept but could not because she was unable to rid herself of recurring malarial attacks. Paying taxes remained a headache as well as pushing the workers to capacity. Grazia had already been invited to travel to Rome, but it seemed impossible under the circumstances.

All this forced Grazia to write to Giuseppe Pinna, an eminent criminal lawyer who had defended Andrea and who, in the interim, had been elected to the Italian Parliament. Grazia begged Pinna to use his influence to gain a pardon for her brother, saying that Andrea would consider himself fortunate to receive a clemency, even if only for one year. (Grazia also mentioned that other Andrea — Pirodda — requesting Pinna to recommend him for a post in Libya where teachers' salaries were, apparently, more generous. Possibly Grazia did not care where the young man ended up, as long as the romance subsided for good.) Her request with regard to her brother's sentence was granted. Andrea came home, but he was on parole and forbidden to leave Nuoro. Soon Grazia was obliged to make another appeal to Deputy Pinna, because only a full pardon would allow Andrea the freedom to supervise property outside the proscribed zone. (In particular they wanted to go mountain-climbing in Fonni.) Grazia's request was approved and Andrea was a free man for the first time in years.

While Andrea may have been legally free, Grazia knew that his imprisonment had left its mark. Even if people in Barbagia were tolerant of exconvicts — for so many men had been unfairly imprisoned — Andrea's self-esteem was gone. He was quiet and apprehensive and he even seemed to be confused. His life was in disarray. From childhood Andrea had been Grazia's hero and protector. Now it was she who was protecting him.

And then came the final blow: Santus, crippled by his addiction to alcohol, became dangerous. In the middle of the night, after a long bout of drinking, his terrified shrieks filled the house. They found him deranged, clinging to the wall and pointing toward his bed under which, he claimed, there was a black assassin. Andrea calmed Santus down, for he seemed about to harm himself in trying to escape his phantom. Chiscedda pleaded with Andrea to send for the exorcist but Andrea, who had encountered this type of "devil" before, told his mother that only a doctor could help poor Santus.

When the doctor arrived he examined Santus and judged him insane. He recommended that he be kept away from his family, for he could no longer be held responsible for his actions. Andrea volunteered to look after him and the two

136

men went to live near the olive press. Every trace of the brilliant young medical student had vanished. In his place was a madman. Chiscedda mourned as though Santus had died and every so often she would sneak out to the olive press with a large bundle hidden under her black shawl. In this way she made certain that the two outcasts were eating well and that they had clean clothing. Andrea came almost everyday to share the noonday meal with his mother and sisters and he would bring Santus along on his better days.

Because of all this, Grazia went into a "pessimistic" period (1899–1909) in which everything she wrote was imbued with a sense of the futility of the human condition. The nine novels that she wrote were all best sellers, even though they were tragic stories. Many were translated into several languages, which suggests that readers, enlightened by various social movements, were also beginning to have compassion for the poor and uneducated of their own nations. If nothing else, Andrea's ordeal changed the direction of Grazia's career and forced her to confront themes that were significant and relevant to her time.

Following the publication of *La via del male* Grazia was also in a confused state of mind. Her provincial life had bored her all along. Now it seemed to oppress her. She was now aware of the true power she had, but the routine of chores, obligations, and village existence left her without perspective. Coincidentally, it was time for the grape harvest that Chiscedda — also in need of some time to herself — had decided she was going to supervise. Grazia volunteered to accompany her. They were driven out to the desolate vineyard by Andrea and a worker who would also help with the harvest. The · vineyard was located on a high plateau overlooking an endless stretch of barren land. On the plateau itself there was nothing but scrub grass and only two huge pines. Other than that there was the sad blue sky, an irrigation ditch, a small reservoir, and a crude building inhabited year-round by Arcangelo, an old servant.

The next evening Andrea returned on horseback bringing a letter for his sister. Grazia was delighted, for she imagined the letter had come from an admirer. Letter in hand, she walked out past the vineyard and over the open plateau. When she opened the letter she was disappointed to find that it was only a request for a copy of one of her books. She held the letter out and let it be snatched up by the wind. As she continued down the footpath, the sky was filled with a blazing sunset. Its crimson light was so intense that each seed, each blade of grass, each wildflower and thistle reflected its glow. The phenomenon washed over her. As the power and beauty of nature engulfed her, Grazia felt that she could not separate herself from nature — she was one with the sky, the animals, the land.

The granite slopes of the Gennargentu Mountains far away became turquoise and the sky turned orange, and then, a deep pink which gradually intensified to flaming magenta. At that point, a ladybug climbed from a bush onto Grazia's skirt, and crawled along her dress as if she were merely another, taller bush. The bug inched its way up until it reached her hand, which rested against the soft folds of her dress. Slowly Grazia raised her hand close to her face so that she could examine the ladybug. To Grazia the closed wings of the small red beetle looked like a human face or a Japanese mask. When the ladybug had reached the tip of Grazia's finger, it spread its wings and flew off into the open, infinite space. Grazia yearned to follow, but realized that her own feet were bound to the soil below. How she longed to be free.

When the sun sank behind the mountains, draining the sky of its color, the heavens seemed as transparent as water. The stars seemed to quiver, as if they were, indeed, reflections on the surface of a vast sea. Grazia went into a trance, and became conscious of the eye of God. She could feel her forehead scrape past the evening star. In that very instant, her ambitions, her vain dreams, her anticipation for extraordinary adventures vanished. Life was perfect. It was beautiful the way it was, even among the humble creatures born alone, among the things created by God to delight the heart that is as near to Him as the infant's is to his mother's.

This experience was a revelation, a mystical phenomenon only explainable in terms of Grazia's own total acceptance of life. Her conscious mind was elevated to a higher plateau. Yet the experience puzzled her. She could not decipher how something so simple could have caused such a powerful cosmic revelation. Just for nothing, only because she happened to see a sunset and the evening star shining over the mountains! The unexpected perfection of that moment made her reject external rewards — attention, fame, glory — and she resolved that thereafter she would derive everything from *within* herself, from within the mystery of her interior life.

CHAPTER
NINE

The events that took place in the plateau of the vineyard were mystical and defy scientific explanation. However, they communicated a solution to Grazia's problems, and suggested certain goals and motives worthy of pursuit. She dedicated her life to writing, refusing to alter her ironic yet direct style that spoke to the general public on a level that conformed with her subject matter and somber moral themes. In her writing the Sardinian milieu became less and less realistic, and the alienation and suffering of her characters became archetypes of universal human problems. For Deledda the question of identity was the most important consideration. From her family's problems — depression, criminal behavior, alcoholism, madness — she had learned about the worst aspects of life. She herself had managed to achieve a certain degree of success in her literary career — yet it had changed nothing; her life remained as static as ever.

In the peasants who worked for her, Grazia observed none of the tensions or conflicts that had torn her family apart. Though simple and illiterate, these people were free, free of the past and free of the future. Living from day to day and dependent on no one, Arcangelo, the old man who supervised the lonely vineyard, was an excellent example. He had been born in Calabria, the southernmost part of the Italian peninsula. He had come to Sardinia as an "exile" as punishment for some misdemeanor. Only Totoni Deledda would give him a job, and before long he became the most loyal of all the family's workers. He alone was responsible for the entire vineyard. Though he was old, Arcangelo was completely self-sufficient, living in almost complete isolation from the rest of the world. He was clever enough to have devised a small irrigation system for the grapevines, and he knew how to make his own clay pots and dishes. When Grazia first met Arcangelo, she was slightly afraid of him, for he was a taciturn, bitter old man. While Chiscedda and she stayed with him during the harvest, however, Grazia came to admire and understand him, and she modeled some of her most famous characters (such as Efix in *Canne al Vento*) after him.

Chiscedda, habitually taciturn and melancholic, felt akin to the old servant. She was able to confide in him as she could with no one else. Perhaps knowing that he had come from a distant place with different customs and mentality helped her to express herself. His lack of education made him seem humble, and yet Chiscedda knew that he was an intelligent man. Therefore they were equals.

By chance, Grazia returned from a walk to overhear Chiscedda and Arcangelo discussing something. She stood quietly outside the door for a moment and discerned that it was she herself that they were talking about. Grazia was astonished at Chiscedda's direct tone of voice, for she spoke with Arcangelo more confidently than she did with members of her own family.

"Andrea is late tonight," Chiscedda said, wondering whether it was the wild boar or a young woman that was to be Andrea's prey in the mountainous forest nearby. "And then, there's that one who goes around like a goat!"

Old Arcangelo reassured his mistress, reminding her that another servant was outside gathering firewood. Grazia was safe. "Who do you think the *signorina* can see here? She is so wise: there's no danger that she's keeping a rendezvous with a lover here!"

"You never know," Chiscedda replied, remembering the incident with Andrea Pirodda. "That one has certain ideas in her head. All that writing. Those evil books. Those letters she gets! And once didn't a big man, red like some fox, come to see her and from far away . . . And afterward, he wrote about her in the newspaper! People are gossiping. She will never marry in a Christian way. Even her sisters will resent her, because in a family the most important thing is to marry the first daughter well. True, her brothers do not help her very much! You know that."

Indeed, the old man knew, but he had blind faith in Andrea. "No, *padrona*, don't complain too much about Andrea. He is good, I should say, too generous. He is too friendly with those wicked friends of his, but, after all, he takes care of his property and he loves his sisters, in his own way."

"He takes care of the property?" Chiscedda exclaimed sarcastically. "Yes, but only to keep all the income for himself. Then he gambles and goes around with fallen women. You call this *goodness?* You call this love for the family? Andrea gives us just the bare minimum to pay our workers and the taxes. I don't sleep thinking that one day the tax collector will come to confiscate our house. There is no way out: one must

142

learn to suffer. But how I love my children! I love them too much. The more they are disgraced, the more I love them and want to help them. And Grazia is the one who worries me the most!"

"Instead, she will be the one to give you the most consolation, you will see," the old man replied.

"I need no consolation, Arcangelo. Nothing exists for me except the welfare of my children. I am a woman without strength and without willpower, but they should understand that. If I talk with you this evening, like this, it is because only you can understand me."

"The roads of the Lord are many and he always helps good Christians," Arcangelo said.

"So, you believe in God? At times, I myself don't believe in Him anymore."

Were it not for the sound of the hoofbeats of Andrea's horse, Grazia would have leaned against the wall of Arcangelo's house and wept. At that moment, she would have given up all her dreams, just to comfort her mother. Every mother deserved the benefit of at least a glimmer of hope for a good marriage prospect for her daughter, but even Grazia knew that everyone in Nuoro had the opinion that she would make a bad wife because of her passion for books and writing. Much as she loved her mother, Grazia could not humiliate herself. Therefore she resolved to leave Nuoro.

The week-long grape harvest was a job done by peasant women. Chiscedda supervised the women and Grazia kept herself busy, at first, reading, and doing some writing. However, she found herself distracted by the sight of the women, dressed so beautifully in their costumes, singing their ancient folksongs as they worked. They placed the grapes in double baskets that swung like cradles from a brace they carried across their shoulders. The women carried the grapes to the cart that would take the harvest to the winepress.

When the Angelus bells rang in distant Nuoro, Chiscedda ordered the women to rest and to have their midday meal. Everyone sat on the ground except one who discovered that her young son had disappeared. The woman looked for him frantically, and soon everyone rushed to help the search for him. Without saying a word, Arcangelo raced straight to the reservoir. The old man dove into the icy water. In a few moments he dragged the half-drowned child out and squeezed the water out of him as if he were a wet cloth. There was a great celebration, and the women, who had always said mean things about the old man behind his back, made quite a hero out of him.

That evening, Arcangelo had the shivers that turned into a fever, but he refused to rest. At dawn the next morning, he returned to the harvest. When the harvest ended, the women went home and Grazia and Chiscedda put their few things together to get ready to return to Nuoro. Chiscedda's next task was to supervise the work at the winery and she sent the other worker for Andrea with a message that Arcangelo seemed quite ill, perhaps dying. Chiscedda tried to talk the old man into coming to Nuoro so that the doctor could take a look at him. Arcangelo refused and in a few hours he seemed to revive. Grazia brought him some hot coffee and talked to him, trying to make him more comfortable. He could read compassion in her touch, and he marveled that someone could be concerned about an old bag of bones like himself. Grazia thought that perhaps the old man was afraid of dying alone, like an old dog. Andrea arrived, bringing some quinine for

Arcangelo's fever, but the old man remained contrary to everything, refusing suggestions of doctor, medication, or going to a warmer house.

That night there was a bad storm. The barrage of hail, the eerie screams of the wind through the pine trees, the rattling window, and the intense thunder and lightning terrified Grazia and Chiscedda. To divert them the old man feverishly rambled on, telling them about the time he met Totoni who had given him his first job, when none of the other landowners would even speak to him. Grazia understood then that what the sick old man feared was not death itself, but that, owing to his age and infirmity, he would lose his job. Clearly he did not mind poverty and loneliness, for that was already his way of life. No, what he dreaded was the prospect of leaving "his" vineyard. Realizing that Arcangelo thought of himself strictly in terms of that piece of land, Grazia reassured him and promised him that the house was his for the rest of his life. The presence of all three at his side enabled Arcangelo to relax and to fall into a deep sleep.

The storm ended in the morning. Looking out at the pines Grazia thought she could hear them muttering, *Why all this? We fight, we suffer, we torment ourselves for nothing. The force of the wind is in vain: everything is vain and empty, and yet one has to struggle because God wills it.* Grazia's own life seemed akin to that of the trees. How much better off, she decided, if man could comprehend nature. Suddenly hundreds of birds flew back onto the sunlit branches of the pines. Sparkling with raindrops, the birds and the pine needles seemed magical, as if they were covered with diamonds, sapphires and emeralds.

When Arcangelo awoke his cheeks seemed cool. Grazia

brought him some coffee which he drank out of the saucer and licked the left-over sugar like a child. Then she brought him some soup and a glass of wine. It did not seem right to Arcangelo that he, the servant, should be waited upon, or that Chiscedda, his employer, would go to the stream to wash his shirts with her own hands. He grumbled to Grazia about her mother, and praised her goodness and her concern for her family. Abruptly he broke off in the middle of a sentence, and rose to shut the window. After swearing Grazia to secrecy, he went over to the fireplace. He removed a number of bricks, and then took a small iron box out of the cavity. He unlocked the strongbox with a key that hung from a chain around his neck and placed it, opened, in Grazia's hands.

Grazia had never been so surprised in her life, for inside the box was a fortune in gold coins. Had the miserable old man decided to spend this money, he could have bought half of Nuoro. Arcangelo offered the box to her. At that moment, with Grazia's anxiety about her future, this was an offer she wanted to accept, but could not. She shook her head, and watched as the old man carefully lowered the box back into place.

Grazia, who had never desired money before, was seized by temptation. She could not shake it and it lingered as if to torment her. It would have been easy to justify taking the coins, for Arcangelo was old, and he had no family. It was obvious that something prevented him from spending the old coins — it was possible that he had stolen them in his youth. Grazia wanted to tell someone about them, but she knew that no one would believe her and they would accuse her of dreaming up another one of her bizarre fantasies. She did not know what to do, and yet she could not force herself to forget the image of those powerful, frightening gold coins.

Arcangelo stayed in his house by the vineyard, and Grazia and Chiscedda returned with Andrea to Nuoro. That night, Grazia dreamed of her grandmother, tiny Nonna Nicolosa. In her dream her grandmother was dressed in the traditional bridal costume, made out of richly embroidered *orbace* with a vivid overskirt and vest, stitched with two palm leaves in gradually deepening shades of green. Around her hair she wore a starched white turban made out of old *nyssus*. Just as on the last day Grazia had seen her grandmother alive, Grazia dreamed that she overboiled the coffee. She turned around to apologize and it was then that she noticed how the grandmother was dressed. Grazia asked her why she was wearing the garments of a bride.

"I have found your grandfather, Andrea," she replied, "and we are now happy in Paradise, bride and groom forever."

In the dream Grazia asked her grandmother to tell her about this grandfather, for she had only heard the strange rumors that he was slightly mad because he liked to sleep out in the fields and to talk to the wild animals. She had heard that birds liked to perch on his arms and snakes would come when he whistled. Wildcats followed him when he walked in the woods. He was so eccentric that people dreamed up different nationalities for him. But in this dream Grazia's grandmother told her the truth, that he had come from a fishing village on the Sardinian coast, and that he had fled from the sea out of fear. His life was full of Franciscan virtue and animals rewarded his patience and love with their friendship. There was nothing magical or crazy about him.

This dream gave Grazia another profound revelation, as intense as her experience out on the plateau beside the vineyard while she was looking up at the stars. Often she

147

asked herself if these "revelations" could be superstitious in nature. She wondered if anyone was actually capable of having visions, or if they might not have been the result of something defective in her character. Grazia knew herself to be strong, however, and she reflected that this phenomenon must have been a gift from God, just as birds are born with the power to fly. This psychic knowledge, this cosmic self-realization, didn't frighten her. Instead, she found it delighted her.

It was not long before Beppa, Grazia's younger sister, received a proposal of marriage, though she was only sixteen years old. Nuoro had progressed considerably in educational matters since Grazia's own childhood. It now had a full program of classes from kindergarten through high school, as well as a "normal school" where elementary schoolteachers were trained. Beppa's suitor was the director of the *Scuola Normale*, and considered a big shot, though he was a stout, flabby man, and already a little bald. But he was a powerful man, so silver-tongued that he had charmed even the coolest buttonholers in town. He had met Beppa at a gathering held at the school, and quickly made her aware of his interest. Almost immediately, he asked her if she would marry him. Beppa herself was taken aback, for she found the man unattractive, yet Beppa also dreamed of leaving Nuoro. Another incentive was Chiscedda's desire to have all her daughters married off. Impulsive and spoiled, Beppa accepted without having consulted with her family.

In a few days the fiancé, whose name was Francesco, came to pay his first visit to the Deledda home bringing books and presents for each sister. Nicolina and Grazia entertained him and tried to take no offense at his tasteless jokes. Andrea resented this talkative, conceited man, but he dared not interfere. No one was satisfied with the prospective husband, but they were confident that since he was admired in the community his status would somehow vindicate all the slanders the family had endured.

On the contrary, the gossip began almost as soon as the engagement was officially recognized. People came to Chiscedda and whispered that Francesco was a libertine who used his pretty maid for his own perverted sexual pleasures. They also reported that he had made fun of Grazia behind her back. Yet, Francesco, himself, seemed sincere and Chiscedda had learned not to trust local rumor. He sent more gifts, flattered his future mother-in-law, and dismissed his maid.

Reluctantly, Andrea Deledda set aside the entire income of the year — from the sale of wool, oil, almonds, cork, ashes, and charcoal — all, for Beppa's dowry. Grazia, Nicolina, and Beppa wove and embroidered linens for the trousseau. Then, one day Beppa received a letter from Francesco, who was spending the summer holiday with his parents in northern Italy, saying that he had just been transferred to another school. This was part of his career, as Beppa knew, and he promised to visit her once more before the school term began. Then he would have to go away to the new school until the time of the wedding the following spring. Thereafter, his letters grew less frequent.

After a long interval, a lawyer appeared at the door. He represented the fiancé and began asking Chiscedda about the contents of Beppa's dowry. These questions were offensive, since they came from a lawyer and not directly from the fiancé himself or his delegate, as in the traditional ceremony. Still, they were questions that had to be answered. Andrea had put aside quite a bit of money for Beppa, but he refused to

149

relinquish her portion of the land and livestock. By itself, this had a relatively low market value, but combined with the other pasture lands and flocks, it provided enough income for the family. Beppa's share came to 125,000 lire's worth of property and chattel, yet if Francesco were only a landlord, the income would be trivial. Sold or put into Francesco's name, it benefited no one, Beppa least of all. The lawyer returned, after having advised his client Francesco of Andrea's position. He claimed that his client complained that times were hard, that Francesco did not want to seem malicious, but to ensure against depriving his future wife, her dowry would have to be at least 50,000 lire, of which 20,000 lire would have to be given him in the form of guaranteed stocks.

Andrea was outraged at the rather hard-nosed tactics of a man supposedly in love with his beautiful young sister. Yet, his hands were tied. She had given her word and the engagement had been made public. If the engagement were broken off, the town would guess that the rift was caused by money. Not only would the family be laughed at but the value of the family name would diminish, making business difficult if not impossible to maintain, for everything, everything, in Barbagia depended on a man's reputation. Imprisonment would not count as heavily against Andrea as his inability to negotiate a dowry for a sister. Andrea spoke as though he might cut Francesco's throat the way he would slaughter a pig. Beppa suffered, and the entire family was upset.

In desperation, Andrea attempted to sell a parcel of land. The bids, however, fell far below its real value. Grazia had never seen Andrea so distressed. She was tempted to ask Arcangelo for some of his gold, but the more she thought about it, the more she feared she might actually do it. Harvest time had come again. To put temptation aside, Grazia refused to accompany Chiscedda. Yet, she was furious with herself for being such a coward, incapable of doing any good for those she loved, able only to cause scandal and gossip and to break her mother's heart. To resolve the issue, Grazia, resigned to the fact she would never marry, offered to give up her own inheritance for the sake of Beppa's happiness. Thus, the dowry was put together. It was sealed in a small box which looked to everyone like a tiny coffin. Andrea was furious with everyone, and when he came to the house his sisters hid upstairs. However, no more letters arrived from Francesco and even his lawyer did not know what had happened.

On the eve of the first of November (All Saints' Day) Grazia had another dream in which she saw her tiny grandmother. In the dream Nicolosa told Grazia that she only had come to bring her own *salutino* or greeting, as well as Francesco's best regards. This dream made no sense to Grazia when she awoke, nor to her family when she told them, for they thought Grazia was playing a cruel joke on Beppa. However, it wasn't long before the lawyer brought the news that on the very night of Grazia's strange dream, Francesco had died of pneumonia. Thus, cruelly and savagely the problem was solved.

The experience of Beppa's engagement demonstrated to Grazia the intolerable misery in which she and her two sisters were submerged. Intelligent and pretty, they were nevertheless all doomed to terrible unhappiness, whether they married or not. She herself began to doubt the possibility of happiness in life, and abandoned her dreams of one day finding love.

Unexpectedly, one of Grazia's novels, *Anime Oneste* (in which one of the characters, "Sebastiano," was patterned after her brother Andrea, and another, "Gonario Rosa," after

151

Antonino Pau), redeemed her. The Italian public had received it so well that in 1899 it was published in France with a translation by a woman named Fanny Rivière. The publisher, Effatin of Lyon, paid the Italian publisher, Cogliati, for the translation and publication rights. Cogliati, in turn, divided the sum with Grazia. With the arrival of the money order from Cogliati, Grazia went to the post office accompanied by Chiscedda to cash the check. With Arcangelo's hidden and sinister treasure in mind, Grazia became apprehensive when she saw the pile of gold coins on the post office counter. Reluctant even to touch the coins she asked the postal official to give her paper money instead. She hurried across the square to the bank to deposit the bills in a savings account. Chiscedda, however, had seen all the money and her expression indicated to Grazia that she thought her daughter must have obtained the money sinfully. Even Grazia herself was irritated by the arrival of money out of nowhere. *"I shall spend it,"* she vowed. *"I don't want to save anything anymore. Let my earnings fly away like leaves in the wind!"*

Grazia had never had so much money to herself before and she really didn't know how to spend it. Every other time she had received royalties from her publishers she had spent them for small items, a scarf, a pin, a fan, once she had had enough for a dress. She had been invited to travel to Rome and even to the Chicago World's Fair. But these suggestions had all made her laugh. There had been no way that she could have gone. Now there were other invitations. The most feasible invitation had been sent by a contessa in Cagliari, Donna Maria Manca (no relation to Stanis Manca). This woman was a real *contessa*. She was the editor of *Donna Sarda* ("Sardinian Lady") to which Grazia had contributed several articles and short stories. There would be no impropriety in accepting *this* invitation, since Cagliari was less than a day's train ride from Nuoro and her hostess was a suitable chaperone. She assured her family it was to be a brief professional journey. Andrea objected, insisting that either Beppa or Nicolina go along, for he was suspicious that after years of separation, Grazia might resume her relationship with Pirodda whose love poems appeared every so often in local publications. (Pirodda was also busy writing articles on some social customs and the metallurgical workers near Buggeru.) Surprisingly, it was Chiscedda, convinced that Grazia would always be a spinster, who overruled Andrea.

Grazia was delighted. She had grown more and more eager to leave Nuoro over the past few years, complaining frequently of her boredom and restlessness. In advance of her departure, she wrote to Luigi Falchi, a distinguished man of letters who lived in Cagliari, to tell him of her plans. "If only you knew what a miserable small banal life I lead in regard to my soul's needs," she complained, "that aside from my family, and the countryside, I would hate Nuoro where misery and vulgarity are more oppressive perhaps than anywhere else on earth." At that point, she informed Falchi, her life revolved around three things: reading, writing, and dreaming. "As you can see, I am satisfied with very little," she confided.

However, if Grazia truly believed that her "small banal life" would never change, she was only fooling herself. It was not accidental that she had set out on a deliberate path toward literary success, and she was as talented as she was ambitious.

Andrea accompanied his sister to the train station early on October 21, 1899, and insisted upon riding half-way with her, making up some excuse about needing to go there for business.

Grazia did not protest, for she realized that Andrea was being difficult because he loved her and dreaded losing her. When he said good-bye, his expression was so forlorn that it was evident he believed he would never see his sister again. The train pulled away and continued toward Cagliari. Grazia had to admit to herself that without Andrea by her side she felt lost. Suddenly all her ambition to escape Nuoro vanished.

The early traces of winter that had already arrived in Barbagia were absent from the sunny southern coast. The cloudless sky was more turquoise than blue, and when the sea came into view Grazia was astonished at its transparency and its greenish, glass-like luster. It seemed like another world, with a completely different climate.

Grazia was met at the Cagliari station by the contessa, Donna Maria, a ridiculous woman covered with ruffles and fringes and a tiny hat perched high on top of a mass of braided and curled blond hair. When the contessa spotted her young guest, her eyes brimmed with tears of joy, and she made such a noisy fuss that Grazia wished to scramble back onto the train and to head straight home to Nuoro. Knowing she could not do that, however, she endured Maria Manca — her kisses, her tears, her embraces, her inane remarks — with the same stoicism that she had learned to endure all the other torments in her life.

They went by carriage to the Manca's mansion built along the broadest boulevard of Cagliari. It was a magnificent villa, with huge windows and balconies all facing the sea. A long marble stairway led from the driveway to the entrance. A string of little girls had been assembled for Grazia, and when she arrived and ascended on the arm of her hostess, the little girls began to sing. With each step Grazia grew more and more apprehensive that when she reached the top of the stairs she might be expected to make some sort of speech of thanks, something she absolutely could not do. She reached the head of the stairs somewhat nervous and out of breath. Then she noticed that the girls' song was mingling with an entirely new sound, one she'd never heard, almost like the low moan of the vineyard pine trees during the tempest. Grazia turned around. It was the sea, visible from the top of the steps. Speechless, Grazia gazed out at the palm trees, the warm turquoise sky, the carnations which grew in the garden, the stylish couples strolling along the boulevard as the strumming of mandolins filled the air.

Despite it all, the visit began with too much confusion to give Grazia any sense of glory. Instead, she was almost paralyzed by fear. Considered reticent even in Nuoro, here, amid the bustling household of the aristocratic Mancas, Grazia was certain that she would humiliate herself by committing some discourtesy before the visit was ended. The verbose Donna Maria escorted Grazia to her dining room for a meal that was entirely too lavish for Grazia's simple tastes. Then, she was led upstairs to the suite that was put at her disposal by her host and hostess. It contained a luxurious bedroom and a small salon, where, Maria Manca said, Grazia could receive her friends and admirers in private. Grazia, however, doubted she had any admirers in Cagliari and became terrified at the thought that someone would actually want to talk to her. At last, Donna Maria left her guest alone.

She went out to the balcony to view the sky and the sea. There was a knock at the door. Someone had sent a large bouquet of red roses. Grazia did not know what to do with them except to put them on a table and then to retreat back to the balcony. She watched some children playing at a game based on the old rite of betrothal, where an ambassador is sent by a young prince to ask for his beloved's hand. In spirit, Grazia joined the circle of children, for it was a game she had loved to play as a child. Somehow she felt that she actually was being wooed by an ambassador on behalf of a great and mysterious man.

Grazia went back into her room and examined the desk. Donna Maria had thoughtfully filled it with stationery and ink and pens. She then sat down and wrote to one of her friends, Sofia Bisi Albini. "I am here," she wrote, "for forty days at Cagliari, our luminous capital, a gracious Moorish city in which the sea with its marvelous sunsets makes one feel the proximity of Africa. I have been having a festive time with friends and I find them relaxing and even entertaining. In a while I hope to come to the mainland and I hope that life, and the world, will open their doors so that my art can fly out to a horizon even more vast than the one which I now see."

Luigi Falchi and his circle of friends were anxious to meet Grazia. A number of small parties were given in honor of the young author. Maria Manca kept a regular "salon" for the "literati" of Cagliari, having a slight preference for people, like herself, who had come to Sardinia from the mainland. She basked in the joy of being the one to bring the marvelous Deledda into her home. One of the first nights that Grazia was there, Donna Maria and her husband took Grazia to the theater. There they encountered Luigi Falchi, who was with two young men from Mantua, who had also attended several of Maria Manca's salons. One was named Marcello Vinelli. The other, Palmiro Madesani, was a government employee at the Department of Finance. The tall and slender Madesani, with his flourishing moustache and his refined features, had a slightly military bearing. Knowing Grazia only by reputation, Madesani gripped Falchi's elbow and urgently requested that he be presented to her, for he found the diminutive young woman attractive and delicate. Furthermore there was something compelling in the way she kept glancing at him. Falchi quickly made the introductions. Palmiro Madesani, feeling that she had bewitched him with her penetrating blackish eyes, knew right away that she must be his. Impishly, Palmiro told her that he had seen her photograph in a magazine but that the original was much better. For her part Grazia thought she had never met so charming a man.

The next time Grazia and Palmiro met was at a small gathering a few days later. A parlor game was played in which each player had to answer all sorts of questions, on a variety of subjects — without hesitation and in such a way that would amuse the rest of the group. Palmiro, young, gentle, with his sharp wit and his soft, sweet laugh, was everyone's favorite player. His accent, his sense of fun, his self-confidence, and his elegance made him instantly attractive to Grazia. She could barely play the game because she felt herself falling in love so rapidly. He asked her a trivial question and she couldn't find her tongue. As a "penalty," Palmiro was allowed to ask her something personal. Grazia waited, wondering what he was going to ask.

Finally Palmiro asked, "Tell us what you have dreamed your future husband will be like!"

Everyone was silent. Her reply vibrated with the depth of her feelings. "Like you," she stated bravely.

Everyone laughed, and the game continued. However, between Palmiro and Grazia there had passed a moment of truth. Coyly she sent him a volume of her collected short stories entitled *Tentazioni* ("Temptations"). Eight days later, Palmiro called upon her at the Manca house. He handed her the book and without a speech of any sort asked her to become his wife. She was confused — for she knew he had a wry sense of humor. To put him on the spot, she said she would accept him on one condition: that the wedding take place in two months.

Palmiro, however, was not joking. On the fourth of November, 1899, they were officially engaged. They took many long walks through the picturesque pine forest on the periphery of Cagliari. There, in the silence of Mount Urpinu, the two discovered that they both felt the same way about many things. They talked and learned about each other's families, problems, plans for the future. They didn't speak with her family about it because they decided that they were both mature enough to arrange things between themselves.

Palmiro Madesani was very much like Grazia and also from a prosperous landowning family. He had grown up in a rural farming area, Cicognara-sul-Po, near Mantua. He loved the countryside, though he preferred urban life. While he was sophisticated, Palmiro seemed innocently, almost naively generous. His admiration for Grazia as a woman was immediately intermingled with his respect for her as a writer. Grazia was physically drawn to him and appreciative of his modest, gentle humor. They were alike — profoundly, spiritually alike.

During the six weeks that Grazia and Palmiro were together, almost everyone in Cagliari toasted their engagement. Soon the news was spread throughout Italy that the "little Sardinian girl" (of twenty-nine!) was getting married.

Maria Manca fluttered about, gloating that her matchmaking had brought the two lovers together.

Reluctantly, on December 22, Grazia departed for Nuoro to prepare for her wedding. There was barely enough time to gather together the linen and lace for her trousseau, but it didn't matter. Chiscedda and all the family rejoiced. Everything was done in the best of spirits. It was to be the first family celebration in many years. In those few remaining weeks before the wedding Grazia felt that her happiness was almost too much to bear. She had searched and waited so long for love, and now that she had found it, she was terrified that something would go wrong. "I fear," she wrote to Palmiro, "that each day which passes in vain will be lost from our happiness! . . . It is time that my suffering cease." In another note she confessed to Palmiro, "They say that my books are beautiful. I don't know, but I feel that with you the world and life have unlocked their doors. I will make my books much more beautiful, which will bring me glory and fortune. I had passed some days in which I felt myself to be an old woman, and everything seemed to have ended. Let us now grow young together!"

Palmiro sent his photograph and Grazia showed it proudly, to her sisters. She wrote back to her fiancé, teasing him, "My sisters found you handsome, only they say that your whiskers are too long, too military."

Anticipating their need for a place to live in Cagliari, Donna Maria Manca, Grazia's pseudointellectual hostess, extended her hospitality to the future couple. Grazia was dismayed. "She never leaves me a moment in peace," she complained privately to Palmiro, "not even when reading or writing. She breaks my head with her chatter. In those hours in which I will have no need of silence and solitude, I will need them to taste our happiness better." Palmiro located a suitable apartment and the embarrassing situation was avoided.

Grazia knew that she would need peace in the coming months because even in that hectic period of her life, she was completing one novel, *Il Vecchio della Montagna*, and beginning another, her masterpiece, *Elias Portolu*. Yet she wrote daily to Palmiro, telling him of her anticipation of the day on which she would leave behind ". . . everything that has generated sorrow, joy, illusion, all which has formed our existence and has thrust us toward the open door of dream. Let us both enter, faithful, secure, with pure and ardent hearts, and make a firm resolution to accept everything which must be. The moment is solemn and arcane. Come, I wait for you . . ."

The day after Christmas and two weeks prior to the wedding, she wrote to her beloved Palmiro again.

> I have come to forget, to detach myself from an incubus of hate and sorrow, to go alone, among foreign people, in a country distant from my own. I feel headed toward an unknown world, alone, sad, drowned in a sea of desolation. Then, at a certain point, I face my small [bedroom] window, watch the pedestrian, study the heads which appear at other windows, the crowd at the train station . . . You think of my being, of my artistic conscience, of my superiority over the crowd, of the occult power which illuminates my soul even when sorrow oppresses it, and I feel strong and invincible in my smallness, in my fragility, in my solitude. Yes, yes, I need to tell you (the rest you already understand) that I am strong, most strong.

Observe in my face sorrow, sadness, each vileness, each misery of life. But the day in which I seem vile or even weak, kill me: it is better to die than to be weak . . . But that day will never come.

She predicted a happy future for herself and Palmiro. To her old friends she also defined her new happiness. Stanis Manca had written making some sort of last-minute apology for a fate between them which did not work out. Grazia replied saying that their friendship and mutual esteem remained as well as their faith in Sardinia's future. She told him that she expected someday to live in Rome. Of her marriage she explained, "I dream a bit of happiness: the man who will give me his name is young, handsome, most intelligent, but above all, he is good and he loves me for myself, a thing which, until now, had not happened and which determined me to marry him."

To another friend she wrote in the same vein, describing Palmiro as ". . . most intelligent, distinctive, handsome (perhaps too handsome) but above all, he is good and honest. We met three months ago at Cagliari. He had not yet read anything of mine and he loved me for myself. For this I decided to marry him."

On one of her last days Grazia bid a final farewell to her one remaining beloved: the wild fields and woods of Mount Orthobene, knowing that forever afterward, though she might return, the wilderness of Barbagia would not be the same. "It is a primeval day," she described to Palmiro. "Just once more I wish to greet the fresh valleys and the savage mountains among which my life has unraveled. I would be selfish to neglect this obligation."

Palmiro Madesani and Grazia Deledda were wed in Nuoro on the eleventh of January, 1900, in the Church of the Rosary. It was a festive occasion for everyone. Newspapers and journals carried the news to all parts of Italy. (One account mentions that Pompeo Calvia, a famous tenor, sang the "Ave Maria.") After the feast, while the guests were still dancing, feasting and drinking, the newlyweds boarded the train back to Cagliari to spend their honeymoon exploring the hills and beaches of the southern coast.

"Such sweetness, to wake in the morning beside you," Grazia wrote in a poem dedicated to Palmiro, proclaiming her joy in being loved, for she was happy, totally happy, for the first time in her life. Palmiro loved her deeply, showering her with attention, tokens of his affection, and tenderness. Grazia was not disappointed that he was no poet, for he knew how to appreciate her work and the work of other artists. Besides, Grazia thought she was not beautiful enough to deserve someone as handsome and loving as Palmiro. If he loved her in spite of her plainness, she would have to love him despite his lack of literary ability. They were well-matched, however, and since they were mature, they were able to support and to love each other all the more for their shortcomings. They were serenely happy and Grazia could not imagine that further happiness could be in store.

As in the army or the diplomatic service, posts in the Ministry of Finance were rotated. In March, anticipating a temporary transfer, the Madesanis sailed to Naples and then, to Venice. "Naples is luminous in these beautiful spring-like days. The women are splendid, and I am beginning, now, to understand the reason behind many of the marvelous things people have told me about the continent." In another note,

Grazia joked about her distance from Sardinia. "I hope to become rich soon and to have a yacht and an automobile for visiting my dearest and unforgettable Sardinia every two months."

The Madesanis were to visit Palmiro's parents in Cicognara-sul-Po, near Mantua. Anticipating that his parents might at first misinterpret Grazia's shyness and habitual reluctance to talk, Palmiro wrote, advising them that, "She talks little and even gives one the slight impression of someone who does not understand. But in a while, after she has known a person, she becomes very expansive. Now her personality is changing somewhat; she is quick, laughs, and likes to joke, never having been so amused in her life, and with me," he added modestly, "she feels as though she were in Paradise."

In April, Grazia's lifetime dream was fulfilled. The Madesani's new residence was at 50 via Modena in Rome. Rome! Grazia was beside herself with joy. The city seemed enormous to her, filled with sights and sounds and adventures. In June, they took another trip back to northern Italy, and then to Sardinia. Grazia continued her writing and despite her traveling finished her novel, *Elias Portolu*. Then when she realized that she was expecting a baby her joy was perfect. "I am happy," she wrote in a letter, "with a happiness pure and serene. My husband is a most gentle young man. He loves me. I love him. We are masters of the entire world."

CHAPTER TEN

For the Madesanis, marriage was a partnership. They were, truly, companions in life. Having married a young woman who was already becoming famous, Palmiro was ready, even eager, to help his wife's career. With his background in finance, he was the perfect agent and business manager. Palmiro's simplicity, humor, and affection were qualities Grazia also possessed, and yet both enjoyed the cosmopolitan life and the excitement of Roman society. Palmiro understood the demands of Grazia's career, and he took enormous pride in her accomplishments. He acted as her manager, protecting her from disadvantageous publishing agreements. He intervened on her behalf in regard to payments and translation rights, even going so far as to learn English, German, and Spanish in order to correspond with foreign publishers.

Grazia's prediction that with Palmiro she would be able to write "beautiful books" came true almost immediately after their marriage. Her first masterpiece, *Elias Portolu*, was published in two parts in the Roman literary magazine *Nuova Antologia* in the August and the October 1900 issues. The first year of her marriage reduced the quantity of Grazia's literary output, but not its quality. With Palmiro's encouragement, then, it would seem that from that time on, she had decided to concentrate on longer, more powerful work.

Inspired by her brother Andrea, *Elias Portolu* told the story of a young man who had been imprisoned for a crime he did not commit. Upon his return from prison he tries to show that he has "reformed" and vows to lead a decent life. Fate, however, intervenes. He falls violently in love with his brother's fiancée. After the unhappy wedding, Elias commits adultery with his sister-in-law. Elias repents his sin as an act of betrayal and joins the priesthood to avoid temptation and to do penance for his sin. Like Grazia's uncle, Don Ignazio, the priest who never had a vocation, Elias suffers great unhappiness. Maddelena bears Elias' child, though everyone thinks it is the legitimate son of Elias' brother. The baby is sweet and intelligent, and as he grows up Elias is tormented by his love for the child, and for his inability to ever call him his own. His brutish, alcoholic brother exercises his authority over the mother and child that Elias loves so much. Elias hates his brother and wishes him dead. Suddenly the brother dies. Not having taken his final vows Elias is free to marry his brother's widow, but guilt prevents him as much as the knowledge that, exept for Maddelena, to everyone, even the child, he would only be the boy's step-father. More sorrow comes when the boy becomes ill and his life slowly wastes away. Elias, "the uncle," must stand to one side, while almost everyone else tries to save the boy. Even Maddelena's wealthy new suitor has more authority over the boy's life than Elias, his true father. When the child dies, Elias feels, for the first time, a release, a calmness, even a joy knowing that death will bring him spiritual unification with the soul of his child.

Elias Portolu was such a success in Europe that by 1907 Karl August Hagberg of Sweden had officially submitted Deledda's name as a candidate for the Nobel Prize. The power of the novel derives from new facets in Deledda's personal life: her marriage, her distance from Sardinia, and, most of all, her impending motherhood. Before the end of their first year of marriage, the Madesani's first son was born at Cicognara-sul-Po at the home of Palmiro's family. Following the birth Grazia suffered some complications. She needed rest. So a wet nurse was found and the baby was left with its paternal grandparents while Grazia and Palmiro returned to Rome. Shortly after his birth she wrote to a friend, "I am happy, happy to be in Rome. Happy with the love that surrounds me. Happy to have a beautiful son (he is brown, rosy with a cleft chin, with beautiful black eyes and tiny, tiny hands and feet). Happy, finally to be able to work with some scope. Everything goes well, very well, too well — sometimes I am even afraid." They named the baby Sardus, after *Sardus Pater*, the legendary founder of Sardinia.

The next years found the Madesanis "rich in peace and in dreams," as Grazia described it. Palmiro was obliged to study several foreign languages in order to keep up with correspondence with publishers who were interested in obtaining translation rights to his wife's books. Grazia completed two more books, *Dopo il divorzio* ("After the Divorce") and *Cenere* ("Ashes") and, in 1904, her second son, Franz, was born — like his brother — at the home of Grazia's parents-in-law. Once again the wet nurse was employed while Grazia recuperated from the delivery. This time she had some trouble regaining her strength and her doctor warned her not to have another child. Grazia was heartbroken for she yearned for a daughter.

166

With the birth of their second son, the Madesanis moved to a house at number 4 via San Sebastiano. Palmiro received some assignments abroad and they stayed in Venice and Turin and, in 1910, they spent nearly a year in Paris. That summer they rented a home on the French Riviera. Every August they returned to Nuoro, for Grazia especially enjoyed attending the celebration of the Feast of the Redeemer. In 1911, when Chiscedda became ill, she came to live with Grazia in Rome, and Grazia never returned to Sardinia again. Her sisters Beppa and Nicolina had come to Rome several years earlier where they met and married non-Sardinians. Andrea made frequent visits. He looked after his brother until 1914 when Santus died at the age of fifty. When Chiscedda died in 1916, Grazia severed most of her ties with Nuoro by selling the properties her mother had left her, except for the agricultural enterprises that Andrea continued to operate until his death in 1922, at the age of fifty-six.

Grazia's sisters Beppa and Nicolina lived most of their married lives in or near the Madesani home. (Nicolina out-lived Grazia and all the other Deledda children, dying in 1972 at the age of ninety-three.) Nicolina's husband, a Tuscan, was a forest inspector who was given a ten year assignment to study the Sardinian wilderness and to make a report on the condition of the timberlands. For seven of those years Nicolina's little girl, Mirella Morelli, lived with Grazia, which compensated her for not having had a daughter of her own. Included in the ménage were a number of servants as well as visitors from Sardegna. Though Grazia needed silence for her own work, apparently she, like her father, enjoyed the household bustle of family and intimate friends, especially those who brought gossip from Nuoro, and to whom she spoke in dialect.

In 1912, the Madesanis built a villa at 15 via Porto Maurizio. The house was located at the edge of the city limits, where the surrounding area was still somewhat undeveloped. At about the same time they leased a house at 194 via Antonio Fratti in Viareggio on the Italian Riviera, just north of Pisa. In the twenties, Grazia and Palmiro accumulated enough money to build a second home in the fishing village of Cervia, on the Adriatic coast, which had a beach, a pine forest, and elegant visitors. "Villino Madesani" was a private place, reserved for the family. It was also only a short drive to the mineral baths at La Fratta and Fiuggi where Grazia found relief from the terrible pain she suffered as a result of two unsuccessful operations to save her from breast cancer. Her last years were difficult, for the aftermath of the operations rendered her left arm nearly useless, and the spread of the disease weakened her.

Before her final year of illness, Grazia's working routine was systematic. In contrast with the elaborate interior decoration popular in that period, Grazia's office was as austere as a room in a Sardinian house. It was about eleven feet by twelve feet, with a window in the corner. In front of the window, which overlooked a public garden, there was a small table. On top of the table were Grazia's pens, encased in a small wooden box, and an inkwell. There was a rustic chair with a woven straw seat. To the left was an old piano and, behind it, a carved breakfront filled with Grazia's own books. She also had a large reading table and some other items, such as paintings by Sardinian artists and Sardinian costume dolls.

When Grazia worked, the household had to remain quiet. Palmiro muffled the hammers on the piano that he so loved to play, in order not to disturb Grazia's reading or writing. However, she enjoyed hearing him play when she was in an entertaining or relaxed mood. Her workday schedule began late in the morning. Generally she fixed coffee only for herself and for Palmiro, because a maid would prepare breakfast for the children. Afterward Grazia would read two or three hours in the parlor. She was a sedentary person by nature. Then she retired to her workroom where she would meditate, searching for the fundamental idea that she wished to express. She based her stories on things she had heard in earlier days in Sardinia and she shaped all of her characters upon people she had actually known, although incident and characters were generally unrelated. Then she would immerse herself in fantasy in order to intertwine the plot with her selected theme. She would refrain from writing until she had been able to work out the concept completely in her mind. Then, she would sit down at her desk. While writing she evoked her country, its landscape, and its people in her mind, and tried to color them in, as if they had only been sketched in her imagination. She limited herself to four complete handwritten pages per day. She would discard whatever did not work out, for she had no patience with rewriting. During her married life she never failed to write at least two hours every day. Though she worked slowly, her constant methodical routine yielded thirty-three novels and eighteen collections of short stories with several additional published works.

Part of her professional life was the social whirl of a celebrity. At first, in her infatuation with Rome and with the new freedom her position and marriage had given her, she was able to attend all the glittering salons of the city. She never excelled in conversation, however, and made no attempt to compete with other ladies in glamor. Her husband was nonetheless pleased that on those occasions when she attended literary salons or went to the theater or opera, she took scrupulous care of her elegance. She was also admired by proponents of women's suffrage and in 1908 she and Maria Montessori opened the first Congress of Italian Women in Rome. (In 1935 Deledda was awarded a unique distinction when a Turkish stamp commemorating the Twelfth International Suffragist Congress in Istanbul depicted Grazia Deledda. Thus, she is said to be one of the few people honored in this way by a foreign government.) If Grazia Deledda supported the women's suffragist movement it was only because equal rights made sense. After all, the traditional role of the Sardinian woman required her to be resourceful and independent. Whether Grazia chose to or not, many people saw her as an aggressive, successful woman. Those who resented her the most were her fellow writers.

Luigi Pirandello was so piqued by Grazia Deledda's Nobel nomination that he wrote a novel entitled *Suo Marito* ("Her Husband") which depicted a famous woman author and her agent-husband in such a way that they were clearly identifiable as Grazia and Palmiro. However, the woman is depicted as making social blunders and being somewhat ignorant and unattractive while the slick husband is described in far worse terms, with the suggestion that he was carrying on with another woman. Pirandello, himself a future Nobel laureate, was overwhelmed by debts at that time, and, unlike Deledda's books, his work was almost unknown. Apparently Pirandello repented, for he never listed the first version among his work and he refused permission for a second edition. Ironically, the revision of this book was the project on which Pirandello was working when he died, in 1936. (The partly revised and more sympathetic version can now be found among the collected works of Pirandello under the new title, *Giustino Roncella Nato Boggiòlo.*)

This book was a terrible blow to Grazia. What was worse, its contents seemed to suggest the collusion of another party, someone who knew intimate details of her life. (The revised version bears a dedication to Ugo Ojetti with whom Grazia had corresponded over a period of thirty years — 1904 to 1932.) Grazia resented the exploitation of her public image and the portrayal of her husband, to whom she referred as *il padrone* ("the boss") in his absence. Perhaps her earnings were greater than his, but he bore all the tedious financial responsibilities in regard to her business affairs. In many ways they were both like children, despite his business acumen and her heavy literary subjects. Palmiro was the more conventionally religious of the two, but Grazia had a profound belief in God that did not conform at all points with Church teachings, for Grazia's "reason" dominated her personality. It not only structured her career and the perspective she had upon the sorrows of everyday life, but it also regulated her own behavior. As a mother she was a trifle distant but, on the other hand, instinctively sympathetic to all the small problems of her growing sons. She enjoyed her sons and they in turn loved and enjoyed her company. Like her own grandmother, tiny Nonna Nicolosa, Grazia was close to her sons in a special way, as if she had remained very much at the level of the child. She once said that in her own childhood she recalled nothing unusual. The only thing that she retained of that early life was a fierce "tenacity" (by which she may have meant patience, stubbornness, ambition, or persistence or perhaps a combination of all four). "I don't remember great events in my life or at least anything different from that of most common mortals

171

. . . As it happens to all mothers, I live life as in former epochs, through the creatures of my art and through those of my blood."

Grazia was always fair with the boys, but she was also strict. She never humiliated them by striking them in punishment, for she used to say that it is better to shoot than to slap. Instead, she tried to reason with them, trying to ferret out their motivations for their wrongdoings. If she found even a shred of logic or good intentions, she would smile and exclaim, "*Già*, they are truly intelligent, these little mischief-makers!" Though she may have been sympathetic and gentle, her dark, penetrating gaze terrified her sons. They could feel her eyes probe their souls to get to their thoughts, their feelings, even their little secrets. When she discerned something there that she didn't quite understand, Grazia knew that there was some deception. Once one of the boys told her that he was doing well at school in a subject in which he was actually failing. With her eyes locked into his, Grazia replied, "No! You are lying!" Her sole punishment, and her most effective weapon, was not to speak to the villain for a month.

Both sons were very bright. However Grazia was not overly ambitious about them, sending them to local schools and even expressing some bemusement when they announced plans to attend the university. Between herself and the older boy Sardus there was an affinity based on the love of reading. When Sardus was a young man they worked on a few projects, including a translation of Balzac's *Eugénie Grandet*. Grazia was proud of Sardus when he wrote some well-received critical essays and showed promise of becoming a great writer. (This promise, however, was unfulfilled, for Sardus died prematurely at the age of thirty-seven.)

Franz, however, seemed to be somewhat resentful of the world in which his mother excelled and which kept her from him. He came to a point where he could not bear to continue with school and he ran away to the home of Palmiro's sister in Mantua, and from there, he went to a school in Genoa. Eventually he decided upon a career in chemistry and returned to do advanced study in Rome. During all this crisis, Grazia was very understanding, for she had not forgotten her own youth and her own desire to escape her environment.

When the boys matured, they understood better the role their mother had played in Italian literature, and they were able to see their childhood in a new light. However, as small boys, during Grazia's hours of writing every day, even on holidays, the enforced silence was irritating. "Speak softly," they would remind one another, "for Mamma is writing." Franz recalled that "it was truly a mystery to see our mother retreat to her office, to take some white sheets of paper from the drawer and to fill them with words in her clear handwriting, without corrections, without reflection. All this had for us children the significance of a ritual. Unconsciously, we understood that in that room, for those two hours, Genius was rising to creation."

Sardus was intrigued by his mother's habits, and remembered more details of the household events. He recalled that she used to laugh at tales of writers longing for poetic inspiration. In lieu of a "muse," Grazia exploited her extraordinary mental powers to meditate like a yogi, seated motionlessly for hours and hours alone and in silence. Occasionally she would move her head as if agreeing with some invisible speaker. One morning when she was deep in thought about her characters, Grazia was heard to say, "Are you crazy?" over

173

and over. Indeed, she was something of a mystic, a fact also substantiated by several scenes in her final work, the autobiographical *Cosima*, in which a number of psychic phenomena are manifested in the character that represents Grazia herself. Her passion for routine and her tendency to use animals in her short stories to stand in for human characters, point to her profound mysticism, as well as her simple style of life, her love of nature, and her attitude about her literary success. She often stated her conviction that etymology unlocked the history of life, fully aware, then, of the complete significance of the words she employed. She wrote deceptively simple prose, for which she was often criticized. However it was vital to her that people understand her message. Instead, her style is so minimal that it could be considered esoteric.

The fact that most of her novels were best sellers demonstrates that her method worked. She explained her success: "At times much can be accepted from fantasy and nothing from fact." Despite the solemnity of her writing and her difficult early life, Grazia had a good — if ironic — sense of humor. She especially enjoyed laughing at herself; for example when someone told her about a new novel that seemed to have a plot filled with love triangles upon love triangles, she said, "Of this, not even I would know how to end it!" Even her reputation as a housewife and homebody did not irritate her, though it was entirely false, and she greatly enjoyed a cartoon that appeared in the newspaper that depicted her sitting beneath a tree knitting stockings. While the press tried to present her to the public as a "typical" Sardinian woman, she admitted that one thing she and her sisters hated was the chore of making bread. And her attempts at embroidery were all poor.

Her own literary tastes were eclectic. She enjoyed reading newspapers and she followed the comic strips. She liked the better quality of mystery novels, too. All she demanded of another writer was that his work teach the reader something about the human condition. She confessed a distaste for the old Italian classics, and when she was older, she came to admire the great Russian novelists, though prior to 1907 she had not read any of their work other than some poetry by Gorky and Pushkin. Much later she began reading Dostoevsky's work, and *The Idiot* was her very favorite novel. When Tolstoy died in 1910, Grazia wrote a eulogy which appeared in an Italian newspaper; though she loved him as a "giant" of literature, she preferred the work of other writers. Lofty, intellectual things did not interest her, and her heart and her tastes remained "with the people."

Perhaps for this reason, she was one of the few literary figures of her day who did not scorn the early movies. Other Italian intellectuals considered film a cheap mass entertainment that satisfied no aesthetic standard. Deledda's novel *Cenere* was made as a silent film in 1916. It was the only film in which the actress Eleanora Duse appeared. She and Grazia had become friends for they shared certain characteristics, not the least of which being their mysticism. The Ambrosio Film Company of Turin filmed the story "on location" in Sardinia, characteristic of the "Verist" or realist approach of early Italian filmmakers. The aging Duse was terrified to perform in front of the menacing "eye" of the camera, yet she felt compelled to take the role for personal as well as artistic reasons. In *Cenere* Duse played the role of the mother who gives up her illegitimate son in order to give him a better life. It was a poignant role for the aging Duse who had actually made the same sacrifice herself. In 1882 she had given her baby, a daughter, Enrichetta Checchi, to foster parents in order to shield the child from her own rather bohemian and restless way of life. Duse's performance reveals the pain and beauty of reality condensed and refined through art.

Grazia's work was also adapted to other dramatic media. *L'Edera*, a four-act play, was performed in Rome at the Argentina Theater on February 3, 1909. *La Grazia*, an opera with libretto by Deledda with music by Gusastallan and Michetti, had its first performance at the Costanzi Theater in Rome on April 3, 1923. It was based on a short story Grazia had written in 1894, *Di Notte*. (Recently, Italian television announced plans to produce *L'Edera* as a drama in weekly segments.) While she may have been alienated from the flamboyant style of Europe's *literati*, Grazia Deledda was a celebrity and she traveled within the inner circle. Even the summer resorts where the Madesanis spent their holidays, attracted only the richest and most elegant Europeans. One summer Palmiro was sick and remained in Rome for treatment, while Grazia and her two sons and other relatives went to Viareggio. Grazia wrote to her husband, "Yesterday the Treves [the Milanese publisher and his wife] came to take me out in their carriage and we stopped first at a chic cafe by the beach where we met Puccini and his wife . . . Treves introduced me, saying that I am his backbone. He spoke badly of all the other books he publishes, saying that they were all brutal, that they don't sell, etc. And those which do sell are not even the good ones . . . With all of this he wanted a collection of short stories right away; he insisted that he have just unpublished ones, but I told him that I am too poor to make gifts.

"Everyone is kind to me, and Maestro Puccini offered me his car to take me home, and his step-daughter invited me to dine: for this reason I believe they do not read my books! Even Signor Dalgas came to the beach and has invited me to go to breakfast at the Foret dei Marmi; all day, people come looking for me."

Grazia was a paradox, friend to the rich and famous, dedicated wife and mother, an artist, and an anti-intellectual. Her passions were art and love. Her life was simple, too, though many exaggerated her "simplicity" into something akin to stupidity. She was modest in one sense, but at the same time proud. She never suffered from a sense of inferiority. She never hid her feelings, yet she expressed herself in an ironic, perhaps typically "Barbagian" way — instead of stating an opinion, she phrased questions, drawing out her companions without imposing her own views. She said she believed in only two things "the family" — which included many besides her relatives, and perhaps refers obliquely to her love of privacy — and art for its own sake. These, she felt, were the only beautiful and true things in life. To everyone in her "clan," Grazia was the matriarch whom they called "La Mamma," and through whom they were bound to each other.

With some critics Grazia became intimate friends, while with others there was no rapport, neither face-to-face nor through her work. She became resigned to being misunderstood and she confided to her friend the critic, Dino Provencal:

> You know that I am always happy when newspapers speak neither ill nor well of my books? I have almost a sense of repugnance to see my name and the names of my characters printed anywhere except in the volume itself.

177

> Maybe it is pride, but that is the way it is. Fundamentally I write for myself alone. If I publish my books it is because this is life's duty: but I was born only to write diaries and letters.

Knowing that disease would shorten her life she added, "Why talk of me? Better close the books and speak of the snow which whitens my hair, a sign that the day is approaching in which only one book counts, that of the active and passive deeds of our lives, to prove if we truly have accomplished anything."

In 1920, after a long series of Deledda's novels had been published, all best sellers, all powerfully written, the success of *La Madre* ("The Mother") became an international phenomenon. It was translated immediately into almost every European language. The British edition carried an introduction by her admirer, D. H. Lawrence. Again, she was nominated for the Nobel Prize. She was among the three finalists, but the prize went to the Swiss writer Carl Spitteler. In each of the next five Nobel ballots, in successive years, Grazia was consistently among the three finalists, yet never a winner. (Those who won were Knut Hamsun, of Norway; Anatole France, France; Jacinto Benavente, Spain; William Butler Yeats, Ireland; Wladyslw S. Reymont, Poland; and George Bernard Shaw, England.) When the nominations for the 1926 prize were being accepted, the secretary of the Swedish Academy, the poet Karlfeldt, officially proposed that the Prize be awarded to Grazia Deledda. This time, she was not outvoted, even though word had unofficially been given that Mussolini himself was sponsoring another Italian woman writer, Ada Negri. Grazia Deledda thus became the only

178

Italian woman to have won the Nobel Prize. (In the Category of Literature she was second out of 6 women and the second Italian out of 4; in *all* categories, 13 women and 10 Italians have been awarded the Nobel Prize.)

The telegram announcing the jury's decision arrived at the Madesani home very early, when Grazia was busy in the kitchen fixing coffee. Palmiro rushed in with the news. Grazia glanced up at him, and with only a hint of irony, said, "*Già*, it's about time," and resumed her task.

The next day brought an army of people to the normally quiet home. Grazia complained about the siege of newsmen and their demands for biographical data, copies of her books, confessions, and even photographs. "I don't know how to defend myself!" she lamented. "A little while ago I went out just to breathe a little." In her interviews she tried not to seem impatient and said repeatedly how pleased she was not only for herself, but for Italy and Sardinia.

In an interview with a reporter from the *Gazzetta di Puglia*, she stated, "Nothing changes in the direction of my life. I shall remain at work; it is not completely finished. There's no need to stop. Today I am determined to stay here in my study for several hours." How different this interview must have seemed to her from that first one in her life in Nuoro with Stanis Manca. She told another reporter that she was working on a new novel that was scheduled for publication in 1928, *Il Vecchio e i fanciulli* ("The Old and the Young"), and an adaptation for the theater of *Annalea Bilsini*, plus another two or three novels which she had agreed to write. But, she stated, her routine would stay exactly the same.

Other photographers begged her to pose for some newsreel cameras. She protested, "Must I do even this?" Yet, she complied, walking toward the camera along the path in her flower garden filled with late-blooming chrysanthemums. She bore herself like someone going out to confront an unavoidable enemy. During the filming, reporters were astonished to see a black crow fly out of the house toward the trees in the park. Grazia seemed quite upset, for the crow, named Checcha, was her pet, a pampered but faithful creature who seemed unable to bear the commotion in his house a moment longer. Grazia conceded that Checcha had more sense than she did, so she quickly said good-bye to the reporters and went back inside to shut herself in her study.

The Nobel Prize is often a mixed blessing. For some it is a distraction, for others, a kind of standard against which future work must be measured, and it is even said to have been given for political reasons. Above all, the awards are bestowed by a body of intellectuals whose literary tastes have been shaped by life in Sweden. Certainly, there are as many similarities to be found in Scandinavian and Sardinian history as between Sardinian and Italian history. And the Swedes might also be suspected of using Deledda and her work as a subtle protest against her country's Fascism. The motivation for the award was not immediately clear to the public. The English-speaking world, having barely heard her name, was stupefied. Yet, once the news was out, there was a general accord that not only did Grazia Deledda represent her own people, but that she was a remarkable storyteller with much to say that was of universal interest and importance. A French critic, Jean Carrer compared her productivity with that of a tree which produces fruit "in the sunlight and in the patient evolution of time."

Benito Mussolini sent a telegram. "Accept, I beg you, my congratulations in this hour in which the world consecrates your glory as an Italian writer." This was followed by an invitation to attend a reception being given in Grazia's honor at his official home, the Palazzo Vittoria. Upon reading the invitation, Grazia's family heard her mutter, *"Sfarzo!"* ("What a farce!") However, knowing only too well that in cases like this duty prevents one from doing what one would like, Grazia accepted.

Mussolini sent his private car to transport Grazia and her family to the reception. "Il Duce" himself stood at the gate of his palace to welcome her. For Grazia, who always suffered each time she had to attend formal ceremonies, the event was tedious. The ballroom was filled with glittering gold and crystal chandeliers, polished marble, and the chattering elite of Italian society and politics. Grazia did not even care for the Sardinian delegates, for her longtime friends and advisors had been forced to retire from politics rather than join the Fascist party. (Their only alternative was a death sentence.) The highlight of the ceremony was the moment that Mussolini presented Grazia with a token of his esteem, an obsequious portrait of himself. For the benefit of those present, "Il Duce" read the words he had inscribed on the edge of the photograph: "To Grazia Deledda, with profound admiration, Benito Mussolini."

This was all pomp and circumstance, *sfarzo*, as Grazia knew, and she could do nothing to prevent the political propaganda her Nobel prize would spawn. She was indifferent to political leaders for she knew most were corrupt. What no one suspected about Grazia was that she knew precisely the political value of her Nobel Prize to Mussolini. (During the time he was in power Mussolini would have the pleasure of seeing an Italian win a Nobel only once more — in 1934, when

a member of the Fascist party won — Luigi Pirandello.)
Mussolini took Grazia aside and asked her, privately, "Can I
do anything for you?"

With a husband in government service and two young sons
beginning their careers, Grazia could have had many favors to
ask of him. Instead, she replied, "For myself, no thank you. I
would only like to tell you that the present owner of the house
in which I was born, Elia Sanna Mannironi, is in exile. I know
him well. He is an honest person from every point of view."

The next day, Elia Sanna Mannironi, who had been
incarcerated in Rome for his anti-Fascist activities, arrived at
the Madesani home, completely astounded. "They told me to
go home!" He exclaimed, upon seeing Grazia, "I don't
understand how this can be possible."

Grazia said nothing about what had passed between herself
and Mussolini. "Why worry?" she admonished, "If they told
you that, then you are free and you can return to Nuoro."

A passport was issued to Grazia on November 26, 1927. It
was made out of stiff paper and it had a flat, harsh picture of
Grazia Deledda in one corner. Grazia's physical characteristics were listed: Height, *1.55 meters;* Age, *56 years;* Forehead,
regular; Mouth, *same;* Eyes, *chestnut;* Hair, *white;* Color, *rosy;*
Build, *complex.* There were a few stamps and Grazia's
graceful signature.

The train ride from Rome to Stockholm was as magical and
mystifying as that train ride she had taken so long ago from
Nuoro to Cagliari. Here too, the seasons changed, going from
the mild autumn of southern Italy to the gloomy chill of
Scandinavia. The landscape rushed by her train window.
Under a tarnished sky she finally saw the smoky profile of the
Swedish capital in the distance: the red tile roofs of the

peasants' homes, snowcovered fir trees, pastures whose greenness could still be seen beneath a layer of frost, windmills, and the stone walls at the edges of the pastures, all of which reminded her of the countryside of her youth.

When the train arrived at Stockholm, and she and Palmiro had disembarked, Grazia found herself dwarfed by almost everyone she saw. Those who had assembled at the station to greet her presented her with bouquets, one made out of the red, white, and green colors of Italy, and another made of the light blue and gold of Sweden. The leader of the group of "giant" Swedes was Erik Axel Karlfeldt, the poet who had advocated Grazia's candidacy to the prize committee. To Grazia, his face seemed loyal and strong, and when he gazed at her she seemed to see the eyes of a child. He was the poet of his land, the voice of Sweden itself, there to welcome her.

Grazia responded to Karlfeldt as one child to another, for she felt that Stockholm was a kingdom filled with fairy-tale people and magic castles. She and Palmiro were escorted to the residence of the Italian ambassador, Prince Ascanio Colonna and his wife, the Princess Elly, one of Europe's most celebrated beauties. They gave Grazia and Palmiro a fine room with huge windows and terraces overlooking the gardens white with marble and snow. There Grazia found a dark panorama of the bay which shimmered with light reflected from boats and houses near the shore. Within the bay were little islands dotted with homes and gardens. Steamboat ferries crossed the harbor, making furrows in the placid, silver water. The air itself seemed to have been made of pure silver, the silence of which was broken only by the call of the crows.

"This silence," she noted, "is sustained even in the busiest avenues of the city; the snowcovered houses, streets, trees.

183

People walk rapidly, even the children who cross the Djurgar-
den Park or who run along the banks of Lake Malar, throwing
bits of bread to the wild ducks, even they are silent and
austere."

Grazia shared her experiences with her sons Sardus and
Franz in a letter that she wrote the first moment she had free
on that first day, December 9, 1927.

> So much has happened in these days that to tell it all.
> (Send me a small pen made out of steel!) I would feel like
> someone who has so many chores to do, that not knowing
> which to do first, just goes to bed. I will tell you the full
> story in person, when I return. For now, just know that
> we are in an enchanted palace, on an enchanted island,
> guest of authentic princes, and even the princess is one of
> those only found in fairy tales: young, beautiful, dark,
> Grecian and elegant.
>
> For today I am not saying anything else: I must now
> receive 10,000 journalists. Dear Franz, along with every-
> thing else, I'm asking you to take care of the house, to tell
> Mirella to [de-louse] her hair [with kerosene] and to make
> Elvira straighten up. Dear Sardus: I want you to know
> that the first greeting this morning to your esteemed
> parents was given along the wall of Servio Tullio by the
> crows who emigrated here to the gardens at Stockholm.
> They said, And so! How did the trip go? Many greetings
> to those back home!
>
> Now I leave a little room for Papa with the hope that
> he won't try to stitch a button there. *Saluti*, and kisses,
> La Mamma.

The formal ceremony for the presentation of the Nobel
Prizes as always took place on Alfred Nobel's birthday,

December 10. Other awardees were: Jean B. Perrin (French, 1870–1942), the award in physics for his work on the discontinuous structure of matter and his discovery of sedimentation equilibrium; Theodor Svedberg (Swedish, 1884–1971), the prize in chemistry for his work on colloids; Johannes A. G. Fibiger (Danish, 1867–1928), the prize in medicine for experiments in cancer research. Aristide Briand (French, 1862–1932) and Gustav Stresemann (German, 1878–1929), statesmen, who shared the Nobel Peace Prize.

The presentation to Grazia Deledda was made by Professor Heinrich Schuck, member of the Swedish literary academy, director of the University of Uppsala and an authority on world literature. He began his address:

> Today in Italy, no novel has the vigor . . . power . . . structure and importance compared with . . . Deledda's work. In depicting nature there are few European writers who can be compared with her . . . Hers is a nature animated in a marvelous way, which harmonizes perfectly with the psychology of her characters . . . In one of her letters she has written, "Our great desire is to slow death down in life. Thus we must search for a means with which to contain life, to intensify it, and to handle it in the richest possible content. One needs to seek a way to live above his own life the way a cloud hovers above the sea." Because of this belief . . . she has never partaken in the political, social, or literary struggles of the day. She has loved mankind more than theory, and in her own tranquil life she has remained aloof from worldly tempests . . . Her conception of life is profound, serious, religious in scope, often sad, but never pessimistic. She believes that in the life struggle, the final

185

triumph will be won by the forces of Good . . . Alfred
Nobel intended that this prize for literature go to one
whose literary work endowed humanity with that nectar
which infuses health and energy with moral life. [In
conformity with this wish, the Swedish Academy has
selected Grazia Deledda] for the power of her writing,
sustained by a high idealism, which renders in plastic
form an image of life the way it is in the island of her
birth and which, with profundity and warmth, deals with
the problems of general human interest.

The beautifully inscribed leather-bound document contain-
ing the last part of Professor Schuck's speech was presented
to Grazia Deledda and it was signed Ar. Augman and
E.t. Karspen. After these words of praise, Grazia Deledda felt
less and less like speaking. There she was before an assembly
of Europe's greatest intellectuals, and she was terrified. In a
solemn voice never before used to make any kind of speech,
Grazia read from a piece of paper so small that it was easily
concealed by her tiny hand. Her address was the shortest ever
made before the Nobel Assembly:

> I do not know how to make speeches: I would be
> happy to thank the Swedish Academy for their highest
> honor, which, in my modest name, it has granted to Italy,
> and to repeat the blessing of the old shepherds of
> Sardinia, spoken to friends and family on solemn occa-
> sions:
> *Salute!*
> *Salute* to the King of Sweden!
> *Salute* to the King of Italy!
> *Salute* to you all, ladies and gentlemen!
> *Viva* Sweden, *viva* Italy!

Following the ceremony there was a banquet to honor all the recipients of the Nobel Prizes. In the tradition of Scandinavian celebrations, the food was as plentiful as the toasts. "I sat between two princes of royal blood," Grazia wrote her sons as if she were still a child, "in the midst of a fantastic court of this king . . . I am amused when after the banquet they pass around glasses of mineral water . . . The bishop of Uppsala, known as the Swedish Pope made a most beautiful address, and there he also mentioned the name of Signor Madesani."

"The Swedish Pope," Archbishop Nathan Soderblom had addressed Grazia eloquently at the banquet:

Dear Madam — the proverb says, "All roads lead to Rome." In your literary work, all roads lead to the human heart. You never tire of listening affectionately to its legends, its mysteries, conflicts, anxieties, and eternal longings. Customs vary . . . to do otherwise and reduce everything to uniformity would be a crime against art and truth. But the human heart and its problems are the same everywhere. The author who knows how to describe human nature, . . . who knows how to investigate and to unveil the world of the heart — such an author is universal, even in his local confinement.

You, Madam, do not limit yourself to man . . . for you, the road is extended. You have seen the road sign which many travelers pass without noticing. For you the road leads to God. For this reason you believe in rebirth, in spite of the degradation and frailty of man . . . Therefore a bright ray gleams in your books. Through darkness and human misery you allow the solace of eternal light to shine.

187

Though the fanfare and the praise of elegant people intimidated her, Grazia's thoughts were always with her family, even the crow Checcha, reminding Franz to give it something to eat. She noted the Swedish crows who dart into houses to steal food, and the other little birds which run around the walls, like mice, unnoticed by the Swedes who seemed unconcerned about the holes they poked in the leather furniture and book bindings. She wrote to Franz, "My greatest pleasure is your news and that of the house: my thoughts are always there, and when they gave me the prize I thought I heard Checcha cawing." Grazia found some things very amusing, especially her husband's absent-minded habits.

> The prince and . . . princess are very genteel and kind to us, even though Papa, despite all my reminders, persists in trying to fasten their stitched-on buttons. I forgot to tell you that the Swedish Pope, who is a grand historian and most cultured man, has eleven children. The crown prince, who still seems a boy, already has five . . . Ah, and they told me that in Stockholm there are no children . . . Now I must get going because I have to dress for dinner. (Here [in the embassy] everyone boasts about Italian cuisine, and they sigh when someone mentions spaghetti.)

Palmiro Madesani was also busy those days, negotiating with representatives of foreign publishers who had come to Stockholm to acquire the translation rights to his wife's books. Grazia herself was obliged to respond to the various courtesies of those wishing to meet and honor her. Still, the ties of blood, no matter how distant, placed an obligation on Grazia that she could not ignore. In the middle of all the events and